# CIRCUMCISION OF WOMEN

Timely, authoritative and persuasive . . . a blueprint for international organisations. This book should prove essential to health educators, medical and nursing personnel, policy makers and all those who respect women. *West Africa*

The best organised and most concise book published on this subject. *WIN News*

This is the best-written publication on this topic. It presents data in a cool scientific manner, but explains problems in terms of concern that any literate person can understand. *Africa Today*

Sound, rational suggestions . . . bring out the originality of her suggestions. *Women's Review of Books*

A persuasive book . . . a bold and instructive approach to ending the mutilation of women. *International Journal of African Historical Studies*

Rare insights and an irresistible interpretation of the World Health Organisation goal of 'health for all by the year 2000'. *African Affairs*

A thoroughly developed model that can be adapted to other countries . . . a wealth of statistical material on the health effects of the practice. These, based on interviews and health records, can be powerful arguments in the swaying of the health establishment to take seriously the need for mounting campaigns. *Women in Action*

I dedicate this book to K. K-T, without whose help and encouragement it would still be in its embryonic form.

# The Circumcision of Women

## A Strategy for Eradication

**Olayinka Koso-Thomas**

**Zed Books Ltd.**
London and New Jersey

*The Circumcision of Women: A Strategy for Eradication* was
first published by Zed Books Ltd, 57 Caledonian Road,
London N1 9BU and 171 First Avenue, Atlantic Highlands,
New Jersey 07716, USA

Second impression 1992

Copyright © Olayinka Koso-Thomas, 1987

Cover designed by Andrew Corbett
Maps and charts by Del & Co.
Printed in Great Britain by Dotesios Ltd, Trowbridge, Wiltshire.

**British Library Cataloguing in Publication Data**

Koso-Thomas, Olayinka
   Circumcision of women : a strategy for eradication.
   1. Infibulation — Africa. 2. Clitoridectomy — Africa
   I. Title
   618.1'6059     GN645

   ISBN 0-86232-700-8
   ISBN 0-86232-701-6 Pbk

# Contents

# Tables

# Figures

# Acknowledgements

I wish to express my sincere thanks and appreciation to my family, especially my husband and two daughters who have encouraged me and provided moral support when things were at a low ebb.

I also owe a debt of deep gratitude and appreciation to those of my colleagues and friends who in diverse ways assisted me to make this book a reality. In particular to Ms Fran Hosken who sensitized African women to this traditional negative practice which affects the health of more than 80 million African women, and through whose influence I was brought into close association with Dr Gordon Wallace and the staff of Population Crisis Committee (PCC) in Washington D.C.; and to the staff of my out-patient's clinic at 20 Circular Road, Freetown; the staff of the Planned Parenthood Association of Sierra Leone, and to the staff of the Sierra Leone Library Board for their co-operation and support during the research for this book. Thanks also to Mrs Elizabeth Hyde, Mrs Sheila Reid and Ms Anna Gourlay, for their help and advice in putting together the final draft of the book, and to Mrs J. H. Carter and Ms Q. Betts-Cole for their assistance in typing the manuscript.

I would also like to thank the Development Services International (DSI) of Canada, Mrs Berhane Ras-Work and Mrs Margareta Linnander of the Inter-African Committee (IAC) of Geneva for their interest in my work on female circumcision and their support for this book.

**Olayinka Koso-Thomas**

# Glossary of medical terms

**Circumcision:**

   *in females:* removal of parts or whole organs of the female genitalia; i.e. clitoris, labiae minora and majora, etc.

   *in males:* excision of the foreskin or prepuce of the penis.

**Cystocoele:** descent of the posterior wall of the urinary bladder into the anterior vaginal wall.

**Depression:** morbid sadness, dejection or melancholy.

**Dysmenorrhoea:** painful menstruation.

**Dyspareunia:** painful and difficult sexual intercourse.

**Dysuria:** pain and difficulty in passing water (micturition).

**Epilepsy:** periodic transient disturbances of brain function manifested by loss of consciousness and abnormal jerking movement of the whole body with occasional frothing at the mouth; i.e. convulsions.

**Ejaculation:** sudden expulsion of semen from the penile urethra.

**Fecundity:** ability to produce offspring frequently and in large numbers.

**Fertility:** ability to conceive or become pregnant.

**Frigidity:** absence of normal sexual desire; used in relation to females.

**Genitalia:** reproductive organs.

   *external genitalia, female:* reproductive organs external to the body, including the perineum, clitoris, labiae minora and majora, and urethra.

   *external genitalia, male:* penis, urethra and scrotum.

**Gravida:** pregnant woman.

**Haematocolpos:** accumulated menstrual blood of many months/years in the vagina.

**Haemorrhage:** eruption of blood from blood vessel.

**Hypertrophy:** abnormal increase/overgrowth of an organ owing to increased size of original cells.

| | |
|---|---|
| **Hysteria:** | a neurosis symptom based on conversion, characterized by by lack of control over acts and emotions, by morbid, self-consciousness, by anxiety, by exaggeration of effect of sensory impressions, and by simulation of various physical disorders. |
| **Impotence:** | absence of sexual power; used in relation to males. |
| **Inertia:** | inability to move spontaneously. |
| **Infertility:** | inability to produce offspring. |
| **Insanity:** | mental illness, where an individual is not responsible for his/her actions. |
| **Keloid:** | a sharply elevated, irregularly shaped, progressively enlarging inelastic scar due to excessive collagen formation in the skin during connective tissue repair; or, an overgrowth of scar tissue, which produces a contraction deformity. |
| **Laceration:** | a wound with torn, ragged edges. |
| **Masturbation:** | induction of orgasm by self-stimulation of the genitals. |
| **Multigravida:** | a woman who has been pregnant many times; i.e. having eight to ten pregnancies. |
| **Nymphomania:** | insatiable sexual desire in females. |
| **Orgasm:** | apex and culmination of sexual excitement. |
| **Prepuce:** | foreskin of the penis. |
| **Primigravida:** | woman pregnant for the first time. |
| **Prolapse:** | to slip forward or out of place. |
| **Rectocoele:** | descent of the anterior wall of the rectum into the vagina. |
| **Septicaemia:** | persistence and multiplication of living bacteria in the blood stream. |
| **Stillbirth:** | delivery of dead child. |
| **Stillborn:** | born dead. |
| **Sexuality:** | constitution of an individual in relation to sexual attitudes and behaviour. |
| **Uterine prolapse:** | descent of the uterus into the vagina and visible at the vaginal orifice. |
| **Vaginismus:** | painful muscular spasms of the vaginal walls resulting in painful intercourse. |

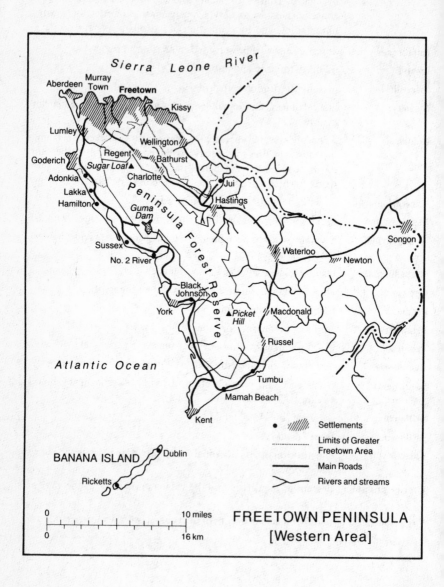

Settlements
Limits of Greater Freetown Area
Main Roads
Rivers and streams

FREETOWN PENINSULA
[Western Area]

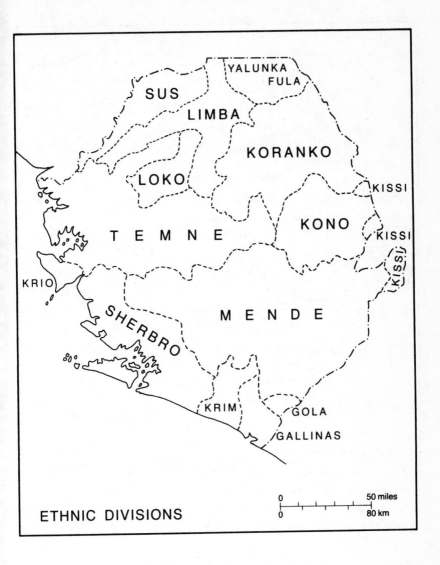

ETHNIC DIVISIONS

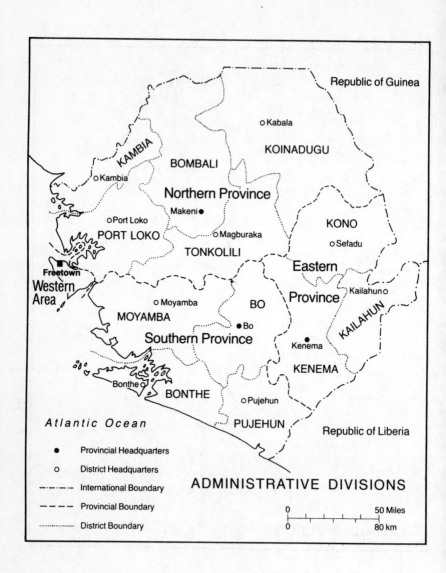

Republic of Guinea

o Kabala

KOINADUGU

KAMBIA

BOMBALI

o Kambia

Northern Province

o Port Loko          Makeni ●                    KONO

PORT LOKO              o Magburaka              o Sefadu

TONKOLILI              Eastern

Freetown                                        Province

Western                                                  Kailahun o
Area        o Moyamba        BO

MOYAMBA                      ● Bo              KAILAHUN

Southern Province

Kenema ●

BONTHE                    KENEMA

Bonthe o

BONTHE

o Pujehun

Atlantic Ocean         PUJEHUN      Republic of Liberia

●    Provincial Headquarters

o    District Headquarters

—·—·—   International Boundary         ADMINISTRATIVE DIVISIONS

— — —   Provincial Boundary

··········   District Boundary        0                  50 Miles

                                      0                  80 km

# Introduction

## Introduction

In most African countries there are certain traditional practices which affect the health of their populations. The greatest scourge, however, seems to have been reserved for African women upon whom it descends with merciless ferocity. Of all the problems traceable to traditional beliefs and which adversely affect the health and lives of girls and women in Africa today, those arising from the practice of circumcision are by far the most serious.

The problem of female circumcision does not fall easily into that category of health problems for which solutions may be found through actions outside the domain of the culture of the country affected. It has a strong religious and cultural base without which it would not exist today, and because this base structure has long been shrouded in secrecy and protected by strong emotional and communal ties, it is difficult to dislodge. The eradication of female circumcision must, therefore, involve the social, religious and cultural transformation of certain communities, rather than overturning or uprooting this base by rapid legal decrees. Nevertheless, the medical and health consequences of maintaining such a tradition have become so great that the social and cultural conditions giving rise to it must necessarily be classed as vectors of a dangerous disease, and the medical and health effects as the offending bacteria. Thus, the transformation required is the removal of the vectors as well as the bacteria to ensure total and complete elimination of this health hazard.

It is quite clear that there has been a subtle manipulation of women in a number of African communities for a long time and the acceptance by women of the situation has compounded the already grave health problems existing in African communities generally.

Because traditional patrilineal communities assign women a subordinate role, women feel unable to oppose community dictates, even when these affect them adversely. Many women even go to great lengths to support these dictates by organizing groups which mete out punishment to non-conforming women, and conduct hostile campaigns against passive observers. Women championing many of the cultural practices adopted by their communities do not realize that some of the practices they promote were designed to subjugate them, and more importantly, to control their sexuality and to maintain male chauvinistic attitudes in respect of marital and sexual relations.

1

Most African women have still not developed the sensitivity to feel deprived or to see in many cultural practices a violation of their human rights. The consequence of this is that, in the mid-1980s, when most women in Africa have voting rights and can influence political decisions against practices harmful to their health, they continue to uphold the dictates and mores of the communities in which they live; they seem, in fact, to regard traditional beliefs as inviolable.

The stubborn persistence of the performance of genital mutilations is but one of many instances of the brutish conditions to which girls and women are abandoned. Others can be found in the nutritional deficiencies in the diets of mothers and weaning children, in the force-feeding of women, and in arranged marriages involving girls in their early teens. These concerns are, however, outside the scope of this book.

# Part I: Identifying the Problem

# 1.  Why circumcise women?

## Defence of the practice

For the proponents of female circumcision there are strong reasons for adopting and continuing the practice; some of their arguments fall under the following categories:

1) Maintenance of cleanliness.
2) Pursuance of aesthetics.
3) Prevention of still-births in primigravida.
4) Promotion of social and political cohesion.
5) Prevention of promiscuity.
6) Improvement of male sexual performance and pleasure.
7) Increase of matrimonial opportunities.
8) Maintenance of good health.
9) Preservation of virginity.
10) Enhancement of fertility.

In order to be able to understand the arguments it is important to have some elementary knowledge of the anatomy and physiology of the female genitalia.

The female external genitalia consist of the mons Veneris, labia majora, labia minora, clitoris, urethral opening, vagina, hymen, and the perineum (see p. 6, Figure 1.1).

The *mons Veneris* is a mass of fatty tissues covering the pubic bone and is usually covered with hair, which forms a transverse hairline across the abdomen.

The *labia majora* are the outer skin (or big lips) of the genitalia; this, and the inner skin fold, labia minora (or the small lip) cover and protect the opening of the vagina and the urinary opening. The labia majora contain hair follicles, sebaceous glands and subcutaneous fat. The *labia minora* have no hair follicles and consist of connective tissues containing little fat, and richly supplied with nerves, blood vessels and sebaceous glands. The upper end forms a hood of skin called the prepuce. The inner surfaces of the labiae majora and minora are kept moist by glandular secretions which lubricate the insides of the skin folds and prevent soreness when they rub against each other.

The *clitoris* is a bud-shaped organ located under the hood formed by the labia minora. It is a very sensitive, erectile organ analogous to the penis, and like that

5

organ has a rich supply of nerve fibres and blood vessels. Because of these the clitoris swells and becomes erect when excited, and it is this excitement which causes female orgasm.

## Figure 1.1

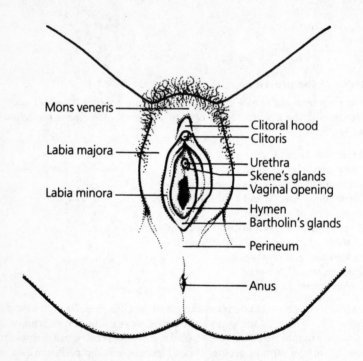

Mons veneris

Labia majora

Labia minora

Clitoral hood
Clitoris

Urethra
Skene's glands
Vaginal opening

Hymen
Bartholin's glands

Perineum

Anus

### Normal vulva before circumcision

The *urethra opening* is located just in front of the vagina. It is controlled by a strong muscle which keeps the duct to the bladder closed. During the passing of urine (micturition) this muscle relaxes and urine collected in the bladder comes out in a stream. The glandular secretions around this area protect it from the excretory products of the urine.

The *vaginal opening* is elastic and stretches during sexual intercourse and at childbirth. In some women a thin piece of skin or membrane — the *hymen* — covers the opening. An elastic tube, called the vagina, leads from this opening from which menstrual flow comes. Secretory glands, called Bartholins glands, are situated on each side of the opening to lubricate the vagina and vaginal area.

The *perineum* is the triangular area between the vagina and the rectum. It consists of muscles and elastic tissues which stretch during childbirth to allow the baby to emerge.

We can now consider the arguments offered in favour of female circumcision.

## 1) Maintenance of cleanliness
Supporters of the practice have explained that the removal of the genital organs promotes cleanliness in that area. It is argued that the secretions produced by the glands in the clitoris, labiae minora and majora are foul-smelling and unhygienic and so make the female body unclean. In communities where custom and/or religion require women to cleanse their genitals with soap and water after micturition, it is thought that the hand used to wash the area may become contaminated by these secretions and this contamination transferred to food, water, clothing, etc. It is, therefore, believed necessary that the glands and organs responsible for producing these secretions are removed to prevent such contamination and to maintain cleanliness. It is a measure of pride in African women to keep their bodies clean.

## 2) In pursuance of aesthetics
It is claimed that as the prepuce of the male glans penis is removed for mainly aesthetic reasons, that of the clitoris, which is homologous to the penis, should also be removed for the same reason. In addition, in some cultures, notably the Temnes of Sierra Leone, there is a prevalent theory that the female genitalia have the potential to grow as do the male genitalia with the development from childhood to adulthood.

The fear that such growth, especially of the clitoris, may become so excessive as to result in that organ hanging uncomfortably and embarrassingly between the thighs of the adolescent girl is said to make the excision of the genital organs important in preserving femininity. Even when there is a more rational view of the limits to which the clitoris can grow many ethnic groups still consider the normal female genitalia very ugly to look at or to touch. This view is common, for example, among the Temnes, Madingos, Limbas and the Lokkos of Sierra Leone, the Bambara of Mali, and some Hausa of northern Nigeria. A flat, smooth area of skin, without the fleshy encumbrances, appears to these groups more pleasing to the sight and touch.

## 3) Prevention of still-births in primigravidas
Certain communities, such as the Mossi of Burkina Faso, and some ethnic groups in Nigeria believe that the clitoris has the power to kill a first-born child if, during delivery, the baby's head touches the clitoris. This superstition has been so well entrenched in some of these communities that it cannot easily be challenged by its members. The belief is thus adopted as though it were a fact. A stronger point is made that the same fate awaits subsequent babies if the clitoris is not excised.

In such communities, circumcision is performed on the female when she is about six months pregnant. If this period is missed, circumcision is done either at the time of delivery, or during the first stage of labour.

## 4) The promotion of social and political cohesion

It is argued that to belong to one's ethnic group and be identified with that group carries with it certain obligations which one is expected to meet before being accepted as a full member of that group. These obligations include conforming to rules and regulations in force among the group and defending the group's cultural base.

Leaders of ethnic groups firmly believe that failure to fulfil these requirements means that any right to the privileges and benefits available to group members cannot justly be claimed.

Identifying with ones culture or with ones lineage group is very important to most African families who wish their children to grow up as acceptable members of their society, with full social rights. They cherish the privileges of belonging and of making friends with other children without fear of being ostracized. In some communities circumcision is the ritual which confers this full social acceptability and integration upon the females. Without it they become estranged from their own kith and kin and may lose their right to contribute to, or participate in, the community life of their homeland, to own property, to vote, or to be voted for. The loss of such rights and privileges may even extend to a male head of a family in which the daughters and wives are not circumcised.

The elders defend circumcision because they see it as a social leveller, being convinced that irrespective of socio-economic status, educational or religious background, it makes all females equal.

## 5) Prevention of promiscuity

In many African communities, circumcision is defended on the grounds that it removes an organ which generates female sexuality and promotes promiscuity.

It is believed that the clitoris, left intact, causes women to become over-sexed, to respond too readily to sexual approaches and may provoke them into making uncontrollable sexual demands on their husbands; and if their demand is not satisfied they may be driven to seek extra-marital sexual adventures. It is, therefore, argued that circumcision is beneficial to women as well as to society, because it protects them from their own sexuality, and from the risk of becoming promiscuous and thereby bringing shame and disgrace not only upon their families, but on the society at large.

## 6) Improvement of male sexual performance

It is believed that being homologous to the penis, the clitoris generates additional excitement for the male and causes early resolution and ejaculation. In many patriarchal societies, to bring the sexual act to a close too rapidly, (although this is outside the man's control) is considered an affront and may lead to confrontation and conflict in the household. The traditional male believes that he should control all aspects of sexual relations, from the initial excitement to orgasm and resolution. It is for the man to bring the sexual act to an end at such time as it may please him, not the woman. Circumcision, therefore, helps to maintain sexual harmony in the household.

In those methods of circumcision that involve excision of the labia minora and majora and suturing of the vulva, the object is to convert the organ into a narrow orifice, the size of which is calculated to bring increased pleasure to the male during sexual intercourse. It is argued that in sexual relations the man's pleasure is paramount and the woman is merely a vehicle for procuring this enjoyment.

### 7) Increase of matrimonial opportunities
This argument is commonly advanced. It is claimed that nearly all circumcised girls who have reached the age of puberty are married within a year of being circumcised.

In those areas where the practice of circumcision is endorsed by the community African men will not marry an uncircumcised girl; tradition forbids him to do so. Most African marriages are prearranged, and it is the man's female relatives who are responsible for negotiating a marriage deal with the bride's parents. These women will, therefore, specify and decide upon the type of girl their son or brother marries, and no doubt community bias will prevail in the choice.

### 8) Maintenance of good health
It is argued that circumcised women are always healthy; that they never complain of any physical ailments, except those brought about by supernatural causes. It is difficult to understand this argument, but evidence is commonly quoted of girls who were always sick, but after being circumcised became healthy, hale and hearty. Circumcision is also credited with healing powers. It is claimed to have cured women suffering from depression, melancholia, nymphomania, hysteria, insanity and epilepsy, and to have curbed and controlled those afflicted by kleptomania or prone to truancy.

### 9) Preservation of virginity
Just as in the case made out for the prevention of promiscuity, circumcision is said to protect and preserve the chastity of young girls until the day they marry, and consummate the occasion.

Virginity, in all traditional African societies, is a prerequisite for marriage. It is highly valued, and its preservation reflects the moral quality of the girl's family. A guarantee and proof of virginity before marriage establishes paternity and ensures the inheritance rights of the new born after consummation of the marriage.

Proof of virginity is usually an integral part of the marriage transaction. It is not uncommon for the prospective groom's female relations to take the bride-to-be to a midwife or TBA for examination and verification of her virginity. In communities practising circumcision there is a strongly held belief that there can be no adult virgins amongst the uncircumcised and so none can be eligible for true matrimony.

### 10) The enhancement of fertility
The case is usually made that girls who marry immediately after circumcision always become pregnant within a short time after marriage. It is believed that if a female is not circumcised, the secretions produced by the glands of the genitalia kill the spermatozoa deposited in the vagina by the male glans penis.

## Examination of the arguments in favour of circumcision

None of the reasons put forward in favour of circumcision have any real scientific or logical basis. It is surprising that aesthetics and the maintenance of cleanliness are advanced as grounds for female circumcision. The scars could hardly be thought of as contributing to beauty. The hardened scar and stump usually seen where the clitoris should be, or in the case of the infibulated vulva, taut skin with an ugly long scar down the middle, present a horrifying appearance. As for cleanliness, the presence of these scars prevents urine and the menstrual flow escaping by the normal channels. This may lead to acute retention of urine and menstrual blood, and to a condition known as *haematocolpos*, which is highly detrimental to the health of the girl or woman concerned and causes odours more offensive than any that can occur through the natural hormonal secretions.

"Beauty is in the eye of the beholder." The eye that finds the normal female genitalia ugly has been conditioned to this perception. Even in those very rare cases in which enlargement of the clitoris and labiae occur, to the unbiased mind the enlarged organs are never objects of disgust or embarrassment.

The tendency to generalize from observations of a few cases can be dangerous and such generalizations should never be the basis upon which potentially harmful doctrines are propounded.

The suggestion that death could result if, during delivery, the baby's head touches the clitoris is absurd and has no scientific backing. On the contrary, so much evidence exists of the normal, healthy delivery of babies from uncircumcised women that no reasonable person who has knowledge of such evidence and is free to assess it will accept this argument.

The issue of circumcision ensuring social and political integration is a real problem for rural families, but the right to belong, to be accepted as a full member of a community ought not to be purchased at such a high price in human suffering. Other regulations and conditions for acceptability in a community that are not detrimental to the health of women and girls should be adopted, and indeed, many such conditions exist in communities where female circumcision is not practised. Even in communities where it is practised the societies responsible for carrying out the operation have other praiseworthy objectives related to the enhancement of members' social rights and responsibilities.

Various methods of community discipline and control already exist within the social structure of many societies, and the strengthening of the women's organizations in order to encourage the performance of their roles in accordance with these structures could provide a new basis for social and political integration in the community. What is required is a reorientation of training for womanhood; away from training for domestic and sexual submissiveness towards training for self-reliance and a meaningful partnership with men in the community. Change does not necessarily imply the destruction of women's societies, as is feared, change should be understood to mean transformation or a shift in direction towards a better life for all.

One of the concerns which circumcision is expected to deal with is promiscuity. All communities are justly entitled to take steps to curb any human failings which may disrupt community life. Promiscuity, however, is a form of behaviour resulting from a complex combination of genetic factors and social circumstances, upon which the retention or removal of sensitive sex organs has no direct bearing. During the course of treating a number of cases at a Family Planning Clinic which I run, it was not uncommon to see young prostitutes who had been circumcised.

A study conducted in Sudan by Dr. A. A. Shandall, involving 200 women prostitutes, of whom 170 were circumcised or infibulated demonstrated that circumcision is no deterrent to prostitution. It is, of course, assumed here that prostitution is an indication of promiscuity.

Prostitution apart, there is a feeling among circumcised women that there is a threshold of enjoyment which they are denied by their partners. Those who are able to speak freely about sex (and there are only a few in African societies) feel the urge to move from one male partner to another seeking sexual satisfaction. From interviews with 50 urban women who had sexual experience before circumcision I found that none had been able to reach the level of satisfaction they knew before circumcision — and were unaware, before the interview, that this deficiency was as a result of circumcision. During these interviews I was told of women who had striven to find the ideal partner through trial and error until they have lost their husbands and their homes. It seems ironical, therefore, that the operation intended to eliminate promiscuity in fact could have the opposite effect.

The argument that circumcision enhances male sexual performance is only valid where males have been conditioned to believe that sexual pleasure and prowess can be achieved only with circumcised women who are subdued and passive during the act itself. The truth is that few men will agree that passivity on the part of the female contributes to sexual enjoyment.

Men interviewed at random in Sierra Leone have confessed that they enjoy sexual intercourse more with uncircumcised than with circumcised women. Several women have also expressed, to family planning workers in the urban areas, their fears of losing their husbands to uncircumcised rivals; Shandall's study also confirmed these findings. Of 300 Sudanese husbands he interviewed (one of whom had more than one wife, of whom only one was infibulated) 266 stated they preferred non-excised or sunna-circumcised wives sexually.

Early marriage of circumcised women occurs because few men in circumcision-based cultures are allowed to marry an uncircumcised girl. The ceremony accompanying the end of circumcision rites is geared towards attracting eligible males, or concluding marriage contracts arranged since the girl was a child. Increased matrimonial opportunities do not occur simply because a girl is circumcised, but from the pattern of acceptable choices laid down by the community.

An examination of the belief that a circumcised woman is better equipped to maintain good health clearly reveals some irrational elements. In genuine traditional communities, women rarely complain of their ailments. Yet the defenders of circumcision seem able to determine relative frequencies of illness between the circumcised and the uncircumcised. This apart, there is such an overwhelming majority of circumcised women in these communities that to find a greater number of ailments amongst the uncircumcised has to be statistically incorrect.

A similar, irrational argument can be observed regarding the issue of virginity among the circumcised. There is no evidence to support this argument, and obviously marriage of women at an early age will tend to reduce the occurrence of premarital sex.

It has been suggested, though not confirmed, that circumcised women can be sexually aroused just as easily as the uncircumcised. They may even react more passionately to fondling of the breasts, which it is assumed may become more sensitive after circumcision. Circumcision that involves infibulation and suturing of the vulva can ensure the maintenance of virginity and can be checked by periodic monitoring. But, for example, in Sierra Leone where infibulation is not performed, there can be no control of *chastity* through circumcision.

There is an unsavoury dimension to the virginity issue, however, and this concerns financial rewards to the families of virgin girls. It is well known that a higher bride price is demanded of prospective grooms for virgin brides. Parents therefore encourage their daughters to submit to circumcision in the hope that it will preserve their virginity and earn rich financial rewards for the family.

The case made that circumcision enhances fertility and fecundity is groundless; in fact, the opposite is true. Circumcision is one of the causes of *infertility*, especially in young virgin girls who develop a pelvic infection after circumcision. The secretions claimed to have a toxic effect on the male spermatozoa are harmless in themselves and serve as lubricating mucus necessary to eliminate friction between highly sensitive parts of the genitalia. These secretions may have been held suspect in the past because the location of the glands producing them are convenient for harbouring infections such as gonococcal infections which can cause sterility if not properly treated.

## Why do women submit to circumcision?

That women accept these fallacious reasons and thus submit to circumcision is as a result of the interplay of a number of factors, which can be analysed as follows:

### The Ignorance Factor

It is amazing how many African females have no idea what normal genitalia should look like. Interviews I conducted among some female patients attending a Family Planning Clinic in Sierra Leone, showed that few of them had seen normal genitalia or knew what they looked like. Most of them know that is the part of their bodies responsible for reproduction, but what this has to do with physical pleasure is beyond them; it is a part to be possessed by their husbands. They had by upbringing learnt neither to look at nor touch it, unless some definite discomfort or pain was felt in the area. They realize, of course, that it must always be kept clean, but the cleaning process should normally occasion only minimal contact.

Most women have been brought up to suffer quietly and not to complain unduly of their discomforts, distress or depression. When conditions pass the limits of their endurance and they do complain, their condition is usually readily traced to supernatural causes. Diagnosis of this kind prevents ailing victims from seeking and obtaining appropriate remedies for their own and their children's illnesses. The tendency of the superstitious to blame all illnesses on witchcraft, results in actions which have no beneficial effect on the sick. Many resort to treating themselves with unproven herbs and sometimes ultimately ruin their health and their chances of survival. There is no doubt that for many years women have suffered far more than discomforts arising from mutilation of their genitals. Their traditional silence over their own personal welfare is a result of ignorance about health matters in general, and this has made them unaware of what a feeling of "wellness" is.

Educational opportunities are being extended to women in most parts of the continent, but unfortunately progress is slow. Also, there is no effective sex education in most countries, and many adult education programmes do not treat this issue at all. Thus, there is little opportunity to teach or show women all the post-circumcision complications, and the implications for their health and well-being.

In Africa there is ignorance everywhere of feminine sexuality. The belief that female response to sexual stimuli should be suppressed, has discouraged interest in feminine sexuality. Sex talk is taboo in most African societies and sex is never to be discussed even with one's own husband.

It is unAfrican to display love in public, both men and women feel embarrassed by it. African sexuality is supposed to be a gift for the procreation of the human species; any outward display of emotion related to sexuality is interpreted as debasing a divine gift.

Some token expression of affection is permitted in some communities. For example, nose-to-nose contact among the Masai in Kenya, caressing of the hands during dancing among the Yoruba of Nigeria. But in general the traditional separation of the sexes in public make physical contact and, indeed, close emotional relationships impossible except in privacy.

**Mystical and ritualistic factors**

The entire organization of female circumcision is shrouded in secrecy, mystique and tribalism. In many cases the practice is inseparable from the religion of the people. Consequently the only groups to escape the mutilating hand are those whose religions condemn it as a pagan ritual. For the majority of the people, there is usually fear of the consequences of not conforming to a system controlled by supernatural powers. These consequences have been instilled into individuals since childhood and include misfortune, ill-health and death. On the positive side, women are convinced that there is spiritual uplift in going through the experience of being circumcised. They wish their children to also experience the same spiritual blessing.

**Disquieting negatives**

In many African communities the female is delegated a derogatory role from the day she is born, and she stays without redemption until her death. The disquieting feature of this is her acceptance of this inferior role which is enforced by tradition and maintained by superstition. It seems that the only place where the female is allowed to exert her own authority is in the home, where she is completely in charge of the family's welfare. She is the first to wake up and the last to go to bed. She works constantly and even harder than her husband. She works in the home, in the fields, market places, shops, offices etc. In most cases she is neither appreciated nor thanked; circumcision is an additional burden. But in spite of the suffering entailed, some women are keen for their daughters to experience pain, bleeding and so on, exactly as they did in the circumcision rite and in childbirth. They also believe that the experience of circumcision prepares a girl to withstand the pains of her first delivery.

The social celebration aspects of the circumcision ceremony can be quite attractive for a girl. She is promised and given many gifts of clothing, shoes, gold and even a trip out of the country. These incentives entice friends, who normally would not be required to be circumcised, to enrol and go through the rite.

Another negative aspect is that most traditional African women tend to have a strong negative attitude towards other women searching for a way to help their suffering; they seem also to object to the growing interest shown by people in the developed world. This interest they interpret as interference in their culture.

These negative factors militate against mobilising national and international support for the eradication of female circumcision. There is, however, no doubt that the momentum which is slowly gathering behind local and international movements demanding change will eventually triumph.

# 2. Types of circumcision and where practised

## General historical background

Female circumcision has evolved from early times in primitive communities desirous of establishing control over the sexual behaviour of women. The concern over women's sexual morals does not seem to have been confined to Africa, neither is the ingenuity to curb or conceal female sexuality displayed only on that continent. It is true to say, however, that Africa's ingenuity in this respect has produced a curb which is by far the most severe method known to date for concealing or suppressing the female's sexual life. The early Roman technique of slipping rings through the labia majora of their female slaves to prevent them becoming pregnant, removed some of the social consequences of sex without affecting sexuality or inducing permanent mutilation. Similarly the chastity belt, introduced in Europe in the 12th Century by the Crusaders was intended as a barrier against unlawful or unsanctioned sex rather than a suppressant acting through any induced physiological change. It is also known that genital surgery took place in some Western countries, but this involved only clitoridectomy, and was performed in order to cure nymphomania, masturbation, hysteria, depression, epilepsy and insanity.

Africa's methods are purely surgical. Circumcision cuts out not only parts of the clitoris but other genital organs also. It is believed that these surgical methods were known in Ancient Egypt and amongst ancient Arabs, and it is known to have existed in the middle belt of Africa before written records were kept. It is, therefore, difficult to date the first operation or determine the country in which it took place. Nevertheless, since it is no longer contended that Egypt and all of North Africa were part of black Africa and once had black populations, it might be assumed that the history and heritage of North Africa were derived from the black cultures now concentrated in Central Africa. The importance of ritual and celebration in the circumcision practice as it is known in the middle belt, however, points to an origin steeped in mysticism and protected by the traditions of the masquerade. This of course runs counter to the iconoclastic philosophy of the Islamic north. It would appear therefore that Islamic conquest in the north swept out the mysticism and spiritualism. Elsewhere it failed to remove them.

While there is no purpose served outside historical interest to trace the origins of female circumcision, it may be noted that many authors believe the practice started simultaneously in different parts of the world.

## Definition and types of female circumcision

It has been emphasized by Dr. Gerard Zwang that any definitive and irremediable removal of a healthy organ is *mutilation*. Female circumcision can thus be defined as all operations involving mutilation of the female genitalia.

Constituted through genetically programmed processes which are identically reproduced for all female embryos of all races, the organs of reproduction, external or internal are thus vital products of natural, human inheritance. When normal there can be no reason, medical, moral or aesthetic, for suppressing all or any of them.

### Types

Three main types of female circumcision are practised: I. Clitoridectomy; II. Excision; III. Infibulation. (See Figure 2.1.)

*Clitoridectomy:* is the removal of the prepuce of the clitoris; the prepuce is the foreskin protecting the clitoris itself. In Muslim countries the word "sunna" meaning tradition has been given to this operation. It is presumed to be the equivalent of circumcision.

**Figure 2.1**

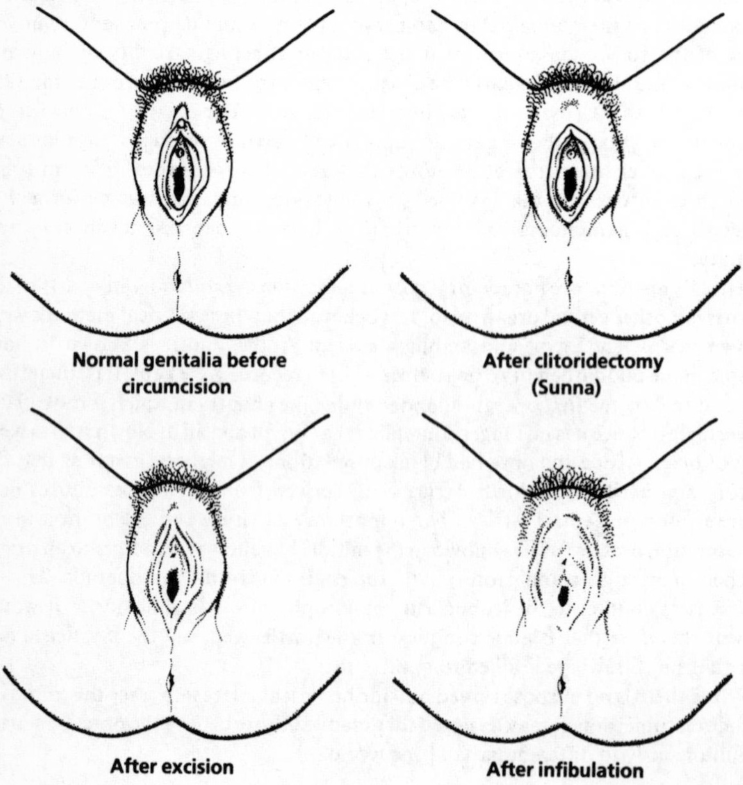

Normal genitalia before circumcision

After clitoridectomy (Sunna)

After excision

After infibulation

*Excision:* is the removal of the prepuce, the clitoris itself and all or part of the labia minora, leaving the labia majora intact, and the rest of the vulva unsutured.
*Infibulation:* is the removal of the prepuce, the whole of labiae minora and majora, and the stitching together (suturing) of the two sides of the vulva leaving a very small orifice to permit the flow of urine and menstrual discharge.

## Geographical distribution

In addition to Africa the countries of Asia, Europe and Latin America practice female circumcision.

*Africa:* Clitoridectomy and excision are practised on the west coast of Africa from the Republic of the Cameroons to the Republic of Mauritania, in Central Africa, Chad, The Central African Republic, Northern Egypt, Kenya and Tanzania; a few, scattered occurrences have been reported in Botswana, Lesotho, and Mozambique. Infibulation is practised in Mali, Sudan, Somali, and some parts of Ethiopia, Mali and northern Nigeria.
*Asia:* The practice is common among Muslim groups in the Philippines, Malaysia, Pakistan and Indonesia.
*Europe:* The practice was known in ancient times in Europe as a cure for nymphomania, hysteria, insanity, depression and epilepsy. It was also carried out to correct clitoral hypertrophy.

Recently it has resurfaced in certain parts of Europe, such as France and Germany where large numbers of immigrants from Africa and Asia have settled. The immigrants have transferred their circumcision culture from their countries of origin to their adopted homelands.

A new trend in female circumcision has been for affluent Africans to take their daughters to Europe to be circumcised under general anaesthesia, in hygienic conditions superior to those available in their home countries. The type practiced will depend on the requirements of their home communities.
*Latin America:* Female circumcision is practised in the South American countries of Brazil, Eastern Mexico, and Peru.

The Brazilian practice may have been transported there by West African ethnic groups who were resettled there after the abolition of the slave trade in the 19th Century. These West Africans have settled in the Central part of Brazil and retained many of their former cultural practices, including the worship of their god *Ogun*, the god of iron. They also speak the Yoruba language, a language of the people of the Western States of Nigeria. It is believed that Eastern Mexico and Peru adopted the practice through contact with Brazil.

Female circumcision is also practiced in Muslim United Arab Emirates, South Yemen, Bahrain and Oman.

It is not practised in the cradle and seat of Islam, Saudi Arabia, where devout Muslims go each year to pay homage to Hajj. Neither is it practiced in Islamic countries such as Algeria, Iran, Iraq, Libya, Morocco and Tunisia.

# 3. Female circumcision in Sierra Leone

## Conceptual factors in circumcision

Various communities in Africa conceive of the physical removal of parts of the genitals as having spiritual significance or associations. The ritual and celebration linked to female circumcision in some cases elevates the surgery from the purely human, earthly plane to the suprahuman, spiritual plane. In some communities this spiritual aspect is emphasized by praise songs eulogizing the parts removed, and in recognition of the bravery of the girls submitting to the surgery.

There are a number of cultural organizations in ethnic communities whose activities are kept secret from the public; these organizations are sometimes referred to as "Secret Societies". In Sierra Leone, for example, female circumcision is usually carried out in such a society as a preliminary rite to training girls for womanhood. In these societies initiates learn to recognize at least two main kinds of spirits. The first are spirits of past leaders of a society; these are the guardian spirits, directing members affairs, and protecting the sanctity of the inner chambers of a society. The second are those of the "devils". These are costumed, masked dancers who are supposedly endowed with spiritual powers. Unlike the usual symbols of spiritual power associated with statues or objects in shrines, these are moving spirits with a physical presence and personality. In addition to these main spirits some communities have sacred objects which are used in circumcision ceremonies to increase the aura of respect and fear and strengthen commitment to a "secret society" and its objectives. There are peculiarities in styles and forms of circumcision depending on the country and ethnic grouping practising it.

## Female circumcision in Sierra Leone

Situated on the bulge of the West Coast of Africa between longitudes 10°–13° west and latitudes 7°–10° north, Sierra Leone has an area of approximately 27,925 square miles, bounded by the Republic of Guinea on the north-east and north-west, by the Republic of Liberia on the south-east and by the Atlantic Ocean on the west and south-west.

It is a compact country almost as wide from east to west as it is from north to south, and consists of the Western Area located around the capital city and port of Freetown, and the Northern, Southern and Eastern Provinces.

## Population and ethnic groups

The map on page xv shows the distribution of ethnic groups in the country. In the last census, held in 1974, the total population projected for 1984 was 4.2 million, of this number 80% live in the rural areas. The Western Area is the home of the Krios, (Creoles), who make up 10% of the population and of whom 80% are Christians and 20% Muslims.

*The Temne:* inhabit part of the Northern Province and comprise 25% of the whole population. An estimated 70% are Muslims; 10% Christians; and 20% practice traditional African religion.

*The Limba and the Loko:* inhabit the Northern Province but settled north of the Temnes; they constitute 10% of the population, with an estimated 60% Muslims; 10% Christians; and 30% practice traditional African religion.

Other ethnic groups in the Northern Province are the *Madingo, Susu* and *Yalunka/Fula.* They make up 5% of the total population, with an estimated 80% Muslims; 20% adherents of traditional African religion.

*The Mende:* inhabit the Southern Province and constitute 30% of the population. 75% of them are Christians, mostly Catholics, 15% are Muslims and 10% practice traditional African religion.

Other ethnic groups inhabiting the Southern province are the *Sherbro, Krim, Gallina,* and the *Gola* who together constitute 5% of the population. It is estimated that 80% are Christians and the remainder Muslims and/or animists.

*The Kono and the Kissi:* inhabit the Eastern Province and constitute 8% of the population. It is estimated that 5% are Christians, the others being either Muslims or animists.

*The Koranko:* in the North-Western part of Sierra Leone make up 5% of the population. 75% are estimated to be Muslims while the rest practice traditional African religion or are animists.

The remaining 2% of the population consists of non-Sierra Leoneans. The largest groups are the Guinean Foulah, the Lebanese, and West African peoples.

## Types of female circumcision practised

The practice affects 90% of the female population and applies to all ethnic groups with the exception of the Christian Krios living in the Western Area. Clitoridectomy and excision are the only forms of circumcision practiced in Sierra Leone; no ethnic group practices infibulation.

*Clitoridectomy or (Sunna):* is performed by the Krio Muslims for both religious and cultural reasons. The practice is believed to have originated from Koranic law and to accord with an expressed instruction of the Prophet Mohammed. Female Krio Muslims account for 3% of the total population.

*Excision:* practiced by all the other ethnic groups in the country is performed as part of an initiation rite signifying the transition from childhood to womanhood; recruits for initiation are thus usually in their teens. In some communities, however, the girls are older and, for example, the Madingo, a minority ethnic group in the North, circumcise girls between the ages of seven days to one year.

## Early history

Circumcision societies are known to have existed in Sierra Leone since the 15th Century, when Portuguese explorers discovered that the indigenous communities living along the Coast and the Scarcies rivers had powerful institutions whose activities were mostly secret; these were loosely referred to as "Secret Societies". These societies trained men and women to serve the needs of their communities.

Because of strict adherence to the laws of secrecy, no information on female circumcision was available until the 19th Century. It is, however, generally assumed that the practice had always been part of the "secret society" training for women.

Islamic influences in Sierra Leone can be traced to the 18th Century when Muslim Fulas from Upper Niger began settling in Futa Jalon, a mountainous area in the north, amongst the Sierra Leone Fula, Susu and Yalunka people. They maintained Islamic law and customs within the non-Muslim people in the area, but in 1725, declared a holy war, the *jihad*, to subdue the three non-Muslim groups. By the end of the century Futa Jalon had become an Islamic state. Those who refused to be dominated by Islamic laws moved south and west. Although the conquered Fula grew stronger again and were able to renounce their Muslim religion, Islam had arrived in the country and sown seeds which were to germinate and thrive in the northern parts of the country.

Islamic influences in Sierra Leone can be traced to the 18th Century when Muslim groups in the country, with polygamy and male supremacy as the common elements. Muslim religious teachings amongst the Northern peoples provided a less sinister and more open framework within which female circumcision could be justified. Also, it presented an opportunity for the operation to be performed outside the former traditional secret caucus.

This development was important for the spread of the practice. Muslim women could, if they wished, be circumcised without the secret society initiation and ritual; yet very few did. It seems that secret societies and the genital operation could not be separated.

## *Bundo* and *Sande* societies

In 1859, a society known as *Bundo* first introduced female circumcision amongst the recaptured slaves from other West African countries who were resettled in the Western Area towns of Wellington and Goderich on the outskirts of Freetown. The society had been established by women from the Bullom Area across the Sierra Leone rivers, and they had persuaded some of the new West African immigrants to join. The loud drumming, dancing and heavy drinking associated with the society's activities, and the growing habit of forcibly initiating girls into the society caused them to be driven out of the community by Christian leaders who did not want the *Bundo* customs to spread among newly converted Christians. Through the strength of the early Christian movement in the Western Area, Bundo societies were unable to find willing recruits amongst the Christian Krio. In the Mende area the parallel society is known as *Sande*, but *Bundo* has become the name generally applied to female initiation societies throughout Sierra Leone.

## Training and organization

Training girls to take their place in the community was an important task of initiation societies and a vital element of women's lives. The training periods were usually for one to two years, during which the initiates were taught housewifery, beauty culture, arts and crafts, fishing, mothercraft, child-welfare, hygiene and sanitation, care of the sick, singing, drumming, dancing and drama. They were also taught how to use local herbs, and to respect the elders and their in-laws: to kneel when addressing them, not look the elders in the face, or answer back when chastized. The time now spent in initiation activities is much shorter and the training less thorough.

Parents of initiates are guaranteed complete security for their daughters, including freedom from physical and sexual molestation. The girls live in the "Bundo Huts" built deep in the forest in an area isolated from the general community and known as "Bundo Bush"; no men or uninitiated women are allowed near the place. The girls occasionally go to the village on errands for the senior members and teachers living with them in the Bush. On such occasions they cover their bodies with white clay in order to be easily identified as initiates.

Bundo Society is not centrally organized, but is run on a personal basis by an individual headwoman called *Digba* in Temne, *Sowie* in Susu, *Majo* in Mende, and High Priestess by other ethnic groups. She is usually a prominent, well-respected, knowledgeable woman of high social status. The number of initiates depends on her skill as a circumciser, her social status in the community, and the number and support of staff she can muster for the training period. She is also the local traditional birth attendant and has considerable knowledge and experience of circumcision and other minor surgical operations. She is also very knowledgeable about local herbs, which can be used to benefit, or harm the community. She is supposed to have mystical powers, and can evoke ancestral spirits, using medicines and sacred objects (*juju*) placed in the Bundo Hut. The fee paid to the Headwoman, calculated on the basis of a sum per initiate varies from town to town and community to community. It is relatively expensive in the towns and reasonably cheap in the rural areas. The Headwoman pays her assistants, and also the area's Paramount Chief for protecting the activities of the society.

Assisting her are senior members of her staff who are a grade below her. It is from this second grade that the *Name* impersonator of the "Bundo Spirit" or "Devil" is chosen. Most women are honoured if asked to play this part. The Bundo Devil, representing ancestral spirits, wears a large, black, wooden mask and dances before the initiates at the Coming-out Ceremony. Occasionally the Devil may dance during important ceremonies, for example, at the coronation of a Paramount Chief, especially if the newly elected chief is a woman and an important member of the society.

The third grade, called *Ndigba* in Mende, consists of all the other officials of the Bundo Hut.

## External Influences

Sir Milton Margai, one of Sierra Leone's most illustrious sons, a medical doctor and the first Prime Minister of Sierra Leone, upgraded the standards of the Bundo

Societies wherever he worked as a medical officer.

In 1928 he instructed the then TBAs in anatomy, physiology, hygiene and sanitation, first aid, baby care, and mothercraft. He modernized the cult of the Bundo Society, and introduced literacy for those wishing to learn to read and write.

## The initiation ceremony

Tradition stipulates that a girl who has not been initiated must not have sexual relations; it is considered most important that at the time of her initiation a girl must be a virgin. A girl found to have lost her virginity is usually seen as a disgrace to her family, her mother especially. The *Digba/Sowie* who discovers an initiate who is not a virgin may charge a higher fee to keep this discovery quiet.

The strong emphasis on virginity before initiation, leads to an assumption by the girls that once initiated they are free to have sexual intercourse as part of their new adult status. Hence the urgency for early initiation. Some parents in the urban areas try to put off their daughter's first sexual experience by delaying their initiation. Mothers, aunts and other female relatives periodically examine their daughters to see if they are *virgo intacta*. Many parents have brought their daughters to me for such examination prior to taking them into the Bundo Society.

The initiation ceremony varies amongst the different ethnic groups in Sierra Leone.

*Krio Muslims:* circumcise their girls singly or in a group of three or four in the home of a relative. Clitoridectomy is performed at puberty or later. As we have noted, they have no secret societies.

*The Mende:* circumcision takes place early in the morning near a flowing stream. Initiates are told to sit in the stream for a few minutes; the idea is to numb the genital area so that little pain is felt at excision; pain comes afterwards.

The *Majo*/Headwoman then performs the operation on each initiate. Using either a blade, knife or piece of broken bottle, she first excises the clitoris, which she holds with a special haemostatic leaf (Black tumbla leaf: *Sialium guineense*, Sawa Sawa leaf: *Gonania Longipetalia*) then the labia minora. Ground herbs mixed with fresh ashes are then applied to the raw wounds. The same equipment is used for several girls, without sterilization.

Loud drumming, singing, dancing and shouting are carried on during the operations in order to drown the cries of the initiates.

When they have all been circumcised, the girls are made to lie down and remain still until the wound has healed. During this time they receive instruction and training from the *Majo* and other officials of the society. They are whitened with a clay wash, dressed in fine cloth, and given Sande names, which are different from those given at birth.

After the wound has healed they are allowed out of the hut, but must hide their heads from passers-by or utter long-drawn cries to warn of their approach.

*The Temne and other ethnic groups:* circumcision takes place in the Bundo Hut, on a mat spread on the floor. Prior to excision each girl is given a stupifying liquid to drink. The instrument used may be either blade, knife, broken bottle or scissors. The resultant wound is cleaned and dressed daily, using locally compounded herbs.

Most of the Bundo Society staff are experienced, trained health personnel, and minor complications such as bleeding, fainting attacks, shock and infection are treated in the hut. If any complication arises which is beyond their competence the sufferer is taken to the nearest hospital or health centre.

The incidence of complications depends on the skill of the circumciser, her eyesight, the sharpness of the instrument used, and the co-operation of the initiate; a girl who fights or struggles may have other parts of her genitalia damaged.

## Graduation ceremonies

At the end of their training, dressed in their best clothes and finest jewellery, the new initiates parade the streets of the town or villages. There is dancing, singing, heavy drinking and merriment, with relatives, fiancés and friends joining in the celebration.

In the *Sande* tradition, the *Kendu* medicine is carried by some of the society's officials ahead of the initiates through the streets. *Kendu* medicine has a dual purpose: 1) it fosters womanly character and virtue; 2) it cleanses and purifies women who have fallen short in this respect.

After the parade the initiates return to the Bush, and are sworn to secrecy concerning the activities of the society. Their heads, which were plastered with a mud "Devil's Cap" are washed; the girls have now attained womanly status. They can either go home to their parents, or to their husbands' homes, where more singing, dancing and heavy drinking continues till the early hours of the next day. The initiates receive gifts from relatives, friends and fiancés.

## Current trends

The educational functions are slowly disappearing, and the training period diminished from one to two years to three to four months and now to one to two weeks. Bundo Society is no longer a preparatory school for marriage; most of the initiates are schoolgirls and must return to school after initiation. In addition, owing to country-wide inflation, the cost of maintaining the girls in initiation schools for several months is beyond the pockets of many parents. Also, all the hands are needed at home to help trade or do housework during the holidays. It is, therefore, unproductive to allow daughters to stay away from home for a long period of time, if they can receive the same training at home at no cost.

Girls are now being circumcised at an early age, this is also for financial reasons. A younger girl is more easily controlled and being unaware of what is going to happen to her she cannot refuse; neither can she demand expensive gifts and jewellery from her parents.

Performance of the operation on a younger girl is said to be less psychologically traumatic. Some of them cannot remember what it felt like, as the genitalia had not fully developed at the time of circumcision. It is known that there is likely to be less damage to the genital area, as a child can easily be forcibly held down thus minimizing movements.

Since the advent of antibiotics and toxoids, some enlightened parents ensure that their daughters receive prophylactic injections of tetanus toxoid and antibiotics prior to circumcision to prevent tetanus and septicaemia. Since the training period has been abandoned, the idea that initiation marks an important step into adulthood is gradually being dispelled as younger and younger girls are being circumcised. What reasons then do women have to continue with this practice? The answer may lie in men's attitude towards women's sexuality. It is argued that circumcision reduces women's sexual appetite, making them docile, peaceable, contented and faithful. Research, to discover whether African men prefer such women, would be valuable.

# 4. Health problems arising from circumcision

The effects of circumcision depend on the type performed, the expertise of the circumciser, the sanitary conditions under which the operation was conducted, the co-operation and the health of the child at the time of the operation.

## Post-circumcision problems

These may be divided into the following categories: 1) immediate; 2) intermediate; 3) late; 4) at consummation of marriage; 5) at delivery of the first born child; 6) post-natal.

Each of these categories is considered below, the symptoms listed and followed by the cause of each symptom.

## Immediate

a. *Pain:* lack of local anaesthesia.

b. *Haemorrhage:* to major blood vessels e.g. the dorsal artery of the clitoris; also due to blood dyscrasias not identified prior to operation.

c. *Shock:* sudden blood loss, unexpected, and unimaginable pain.

d. *Acute urinary retention:* due to: i) pain and burning sensation of urine on the raw wound; ii) fear of passing urine on the raw genitalia; iii) damage to the urethra and its surrounding tissue; the urethra opening closes by reflex action; iv) labial adhesion; v) complete closure of the vaginal orifice by the circumcision scar, common in infibulation.

e. *Urinary infection:* urine retention, the use of unsterilized equipment and the application of local dressings of cowdung and ashes. The infecting organisms ascend through the short urethra into the bladder, and then the kidneys.

f. *Septicaemia (blood poisoning):* the operation being performed in unhygienic conditions, coupled with the use of unsterilized equipment and the application of herbs and ashes to the wound.

g. *Fever:* septicaemia; acute retention of urine; lack of availability and administration of antibiotics.

h. *Tetanus:* use of unsterilized equipment and lack of proper, sterilized hospital wound dressings. Lack of tetanus toxoid injection.

i. *Death:* shock, haemorrhage, tetanus, lack of availability of medical services.

Delay in seeking medical help.

j. *Fractured clavicle, femur, or humerus:* heavy pressure applied to the struggling girl.

## Intermediate

*Delay in wound healing:* infection, anaemia and malnutrition.

*Pelvic infection:* infection of the uterus and vagina from the infected genital wound.

*Dysmenorrhoea:* tight circumcision or keloid scar obstructing the vaginal orifice; pelvic infection or pelvic congestion.

*Cysts and abscesses:* edges of incision being turned inwards and damage to Bartholin's duct. The duct's mucous secretion accumulates forming cysts which later become infected and form abscesses on the vulva. Very common in infibulation.

*Keloid scar:* slow and incomplete healing of the wound, and infection after the operation leading to production of excess connective tissues in the scar.

*Dyspareunia or painful intercourse:* tight vaginal opening or pelvic infection and injury to the vulva area caused by repeated vigorous sexual acts. Also due to vaginismus.

## Late complications

*Haematocolpos:* closure of the vaginal opening by the scar tissue. The menstrual blood accumulates over many months in the vagina and uterus. It appears as a bluish, bulging membrane on vaginal examination.

*Infertility:* chronic pelvic infection blocking both Fallopian tubes — undiagnosed and untreated until it is too late. Also vaginal or rectal fistulae causing frequent miscarriages, making it difficult for the woman to produce a live child.

*Recurrent urinary tract infection:* urinary opening being covered by scar tissue or flap of skin, due to inadequate treatment at time of circumcision and lack of medical facilities. Ignorance of the cause of illness. Lack of cleanliness owing to difficulty in getting around urethral opening, allowing micro-organisms to develop and ascend through the urethral opening into the bladder. Stasis of urine in the bladder. Inability to completely evacuate bladder.

*Difficulty in urinating:* damaged urethral opening and scarring over this opening at excision and infibulation.

*Calculus/stone formation:* scar tissue obstructing urethral opening, and stasis of urine coupled with bacterial infection.

*Hypersensitivity:* development of neuroma on the dorsal nerve of the clitoris.

*Anal incontinence and fissure:* rectal intercourse when vaginal intercourse is not possible. Vaginal opening is too small and husband becomes desperate and frustrated.

## Consummation

*Difficulty in penetration:* pin-hole vaginal orifice/tight circumcision.

*Dyspareunia:* rigid scar tissue; anxiety and fear of the sex act and of the cutting of infibulation scar with a sharp instrument.

*False Vagina:* failure of the circumcision scar to dilate.

## At delivery

**1) Mother:** *prolonged and obstructed labour:* tough, unyielding circumcision scar.
*Haemorrhage, leading to shock and death:* tearing of the scar tissue or the uterine cervix.
*Unnecessary Caesarian sections:* occurs in Europe where the doctors are not familiar with the circumcision.
*Perineal laceration:* head of baby being pushed through the perineum.
*Uterine inertia:* excessive blood loss and pain during the second stage of labour.
*Other obstetrical consequences:* Difficulty in performing a good pelvic examination during labour, leading to wrong monitoring of the stage of delivery and wrong foetal presentation, which may result in a difficult birth.
*Other gynaecological consequences:* Difficulty in performing a good vaginal examination, and thus missing important gynaecological diagnosis, which may affect the patient's health. For example: it is impossible to insert a speculum and take Pap's smear to test for cancer of the cervix, or to insert an IUD, or perform other pelvic examination without cutting the infibulation scar and subjecting the woman to more pain, bleeding and potential infection, sepsis and delayed healing.

**2) Child:** *Still-born:* prolonged, obstructed labour and lack of oxygen in the vaginal canal; *or* if a live birth, the lack of oxygen results in *brain damage* and consequently a *mentally handicapped* individual. Damage to the head or face during delivery by untrained local midwife, or Traditional Birth Attendant (TBA).

## Post-natal complications

*Fistulae — urinary and rectal:* obstructed labour due to necrosis of the vaginal wall, caused by constant pressure of the baby's head on the posterior wall of the urinary bladder and the anterior wall of the rectum during prolonged labour.

Both conditions are very disturbing to the patients who suffer from them. Some are very upset as they constantly smell of urine; others suffer frequent miscarriages as urine usually seeps through the cervical os and poisons the growing foetus.

*Prolapse:* consists of rectocele and cystocele (see below).
*Rectocele and Cystocele:* prolonged labour, pushing of the baby's head during labour and delivery in multigravida (frequent pregnancies), often resulting in prolapse which is the descent of the uterus into the vagina and sometimes through the vulva orifice, with or without adjacent pelvic visceral structures —bladder or rectalcolon.

## Sexual problems

*Lack of orgasm:* amputation of the *glans clitoris.*
*Frigidity:* dyspareunia, injuries sustained during early intercourse. Pelvic infection.
*Anxiety:* inbuilt sense of inadequacy to effectively respond to, and satisfy their husband's emotional needs.

*Depression:* owing to recurring episodes of frigidity and anxiety.

These two conditions may lead to mild or moderate psychosis, especially when jealousy of a potential rival for their husband's affection arises.

*Temporary impotence and frustration:* lack of penetration; inability to consummate marriage after many days or weeks.

# 5. Humane management of post-circumcised women

Women who undergo circumcision suffer to various degrees emotional and mental distress depending on the nature of the mutilation and the resultant medical condition. It is important, therefore, to have a full understanding of the emotional state of the patients during examination to ensure that this invisible condition is relieved as much as possible rather than aggravated. Treatment must also be given which aims at complete rehabilitation of the individual.

Circumcision is often accompanied by severe pain, bleeding, vaginal and urinary infection, and in a few cases results in death. Symptoms which go unnoticed are mental depression, frigidity and mental disorder.

Immediate current medical treatment consists of alleviating severe pain, controlling excessive bleeding and sepsis, and managing any other genital mutilation. The more serious damage suffered by the victim has generally been left unattended in Sierra Leone hospitals.

## Casualties
Records of the casualties resulting from circumcision are not available for the whole country. Not all cases report to recognized hospitals and when they do, several ask for secrecy to be maintained. A study of 100 circumcised girls from a small rural village in the mountains overlooking Freetown, the capital city, show how serious the problem is when extrapolated to obtain the incidence in the whole country.

The girls, aged 8–12 years, were examined over a period of two years at a small clinic in Freetown. Referrals were made to a children's hospital when the condition of the children indicated this was necessary. Table 5.1 gives a breakdown of symptoms displayed and number involved.

This record shows that 83% of all females undergoing circumcision are likely to be affected by some condition requiring medical attention at some time during their life. There are, of course, several communities in the country without modern medical facilities and where emergencies arising from circumcision cannot be treated. In such circumstances a child developing uncontrolled bleeding or infection after circumcision may die within hours of the operation.

Physicians who have investigated cases of circumcision have given various reasons for the incidence of infection. These include: 1) use of unsterilized equipment; 2) lack of care in aseptically preparing the genital area; 3) application of harmful local medicinal preparations to the wound; 4) no significant post-surgical care.

Table 5.1

**Health problems**

| Type and Symptoms | Number Affected | Number Hospitalised | Deaths |
|---|---|---|---|
| **Emergencies:** | | | |
| Vaginal bleeding | 10 | | |
| Pain | 8–10 | 12 | 1 |
| Acute urine retention | 8 | | |
| Tetanus | 5 | | |
| **Ordinary:** | | | |
| Vaginal discharge | 50 | | |
| Dysuria | 15 | | |
| No obvious clinical symptoms | 17 | | |

It has been observed that as girls grow older some of the symptoms first identified after circumcision recur in adolescence and new symptoms also come to light. The most common of these are dysmenorrhoea, and dyspareunia, which leads to frigidity and to serious mental disturbance. Housewives in this category, particularly those in polygamous communities, tend to lose interest in life as they realize that they can no longer hold their husbands' interest and affection which may be transferred to their other wives. Such cases add further to existing mental health problems in the country.

Women who are expecting their first delivery fall into a high risk group. They may develop urinary fistula after delivery, as scarred vulva tissues narrow the external opening of the vagina and make labour prolonged and difficult. This condition is extremely distressing, as the women who suffer from it constantly smell of urine and become social outcasts, even amongst those who adhere to traditions which protect the system that caused their condition. Some of these women are never able to produce a live child at term, others suffer from frequent miscarriages during the first trimester as a result of infected urine escaping from the urinary tract into the uterus. Others, overcome by the hopelessness of their condition, may take their own lives.

No statistical data is available for Sierra Leone as a whole, but data collected by the Family Planning Clinic in Freetown indicate that 5–10% of women seen annually suffer from this condition. In addition, it has been found that the incidence of obstructed labour is quite high in those areas of the country where the practice of circumcision is prevalent.

The victims of circumcision come from all walks of life and from varying social backgrounds. The strongest adherents to the ritual, however, are amongst the non-Christian ethnic groups, and these groups form the majority of the female population. For them there seems no escape. These women and female children live under the yoke of fear, anxiety, pain and mental distress in communities which compel them to believe in the nobility of the social and religious causes for which they sacrifice their health and well-being.

## The humane approach to treatment

There are two risk groups to be considered:
1. Women and girls who are faithful adherents to the belief that circumcision is an inseparable part of the culture and religion of their people. This group accepts the consequences of the practice as a price to be paid for preserving cultural integrity.
2. Women and girls kidnapped and forced against their will to undergo circumcision.

Those in the first group could be treated in hospitals and clinics for ordinarily recognizable post-circumcision symptoms, without seriously upsetting their mental states. Such hospitals in Sierra Leone do not have counselling facilities.

Patients are seen in a routine fashion, ailments diagnosed and treatment prescribed in a rather soulless manner. Hospitals and clinics are crowded and each patient is allotted a minimum consulting time. Such routine treatment works for non-recurrent symptoms; patients in this category are almost certain to have had intensive religious and cultural training in secret societies preceding circumcision, and have been prepared to accept any resultant suffering as the will of a Divine Power. Such patients leave hospitals free from any emotional or psychological damage.

When symptoms are recurrent, however, and when serious conditions lead to a permanent disability, the treatment in general hospitals and clinics has proved to be inadequate. Between December 1981 and October 1982 550 patients were investigated at a private clinic, all of whom had made between five and six hospital visits over the previous three years without seeing any improvement in their condition. The distribution of cases according to types of symptoms is shown in Table 5.2.

Table 5.2

**Health problems**

| Symptoms | No | Treatment |
|---|---|---|
| Dysuria and urinary infection | 300 | Medical |
| Vaginal discharge | 200 | Medical |
| Dyspareunia | 50 | Surgical intervention by referral |
| Pain | 550 | Analgesic drugs given |

In all these cases, long sessions were held with individual patients in which circumcision was generally discussed, explanations given of the reasons for their conditions, and confidence inspired in them about the chances of leading a full and normal life. The treatment to be given was explained and the patient encouraged to follow it with confidence, even when surgery was required. Patients were encouraged to call at the clinic whenever they felt disturbed about their condition or any aspect of their treatment.

By the end of the period a reported cure rate of 85% was achieved. Even where there was failure the attitude developed among the patients through this special caring technique provided the additional strength needed to supplement their religious teachings on the value and purposefulness of life.

Those in the second group who are taken into hospitals and clinics with post-circumcision symptoms develop serious mental problems. They arrive in a condition of shock, some are extremely agitated and deeply suspicious of anyone attempting to treat them. There are no facilities to handle such cases in the general hospitals and the results of treatment of these patients have been disastrous. Documentary evidence on these cases is very sketchy, and only recently has some organised work been proposed by a newly formed Committee on Female Circumcision.

In a number of cases casualties are taken directly to private clinics, rather than public hospitals, in order to avoid any adverse publicity arising from the patient's uncontrolled reaction. Patients in this category who are able to see a physician either at a public hospital or a private clinic must count themselves as the most fortunate of their group. For many, the repercussion of protesting against circumcision and being forced to succumb to it are very grave indeed. Any resulting illness is readily looked upon as God's vengeance upon a disobedient follower, and treatment may be denied the patient.

Appeals for treatment are at two levels: 1) from remorseful parents, guardians and circumcisers; 2) in emergencies.

Some parents or guardians who notice signs of withdrawal from normal family activities of a girl who has recently undergone circumcision — apparently without any ill-effects — become concerned and seek help from a private clinic. But, it has been observed that not all private clinics have been of help. Many doctors are impatient when dealing with problems arising from cultural and religious practices and are apt to be openly critical of the culture. Such behaviour increases the rift between parents and forcibly circumcised patients and may increase the pain and humiliation experienced by girls who have been subjected to the ordeal against their will.

The approach to treating cases of this nature must be positive rather than negative. Any attempt to lay blame on any of the involved parties must be resisted. The experiences of parents has been that women doctors have a greater flair and sensitivity in handling such cases.

Obviously a woman doctor feels anger against the executors of the ritual, and sadness at the futility of the exercise and the stubbornness of the traditional communities. But, above all this, the determination to rescue a life poised at the brink of destruction must dominate. It generally requires great skill and tact to accomplish such a rescue operation. In African communities, no matter how desperate the patient's emotional state, it is essential not to resort too quickly to a referral which will entail open consultation with a psychiatrist, because the patient and her relatives will then assume that the case has gone beyond redemption, and more importantly, the patient's response to treatment will be diminished.

With successful handling of the initial emotional problems the physical disabilities and infections can be treated with greater success.

Conditions needing emergency treatment are often brought to the attention of private clinics. Such emergencies arise as a result of: 1) severe uncontrolled bleeding; 2) infection; 3) acute retention of urine.

These patients are treated immediately they arrive and then sent home. There remains the problem of emotional distress, but this calls for a different approach from that required for the former category of patients. We refer to this as the "Dive and Surface Technique". It is extremely difficult and even dangerous to attempt to do more than a little at a time.

The next step is to invite the parents or guardians to the clinic for discussion without their children. During this session the health hazards attendant upon circumcision are explained, including the dangers to the lives of their children and the possibility of the destruction of their womanhood. Care is taken to avoid reference to elements of their culture, which they may find objectionable, or to any statements calling for the rejection of their culture. The emphasis is placed on the degree of suffering associated with circumcision and the natural reaction of children to such sufferings. No matter how strong their religious commitments, it is sometimes possible to obtain some understanding of the reluctant child's position and to persuade many of the women to realize the importance of maintaining social dignity for women. Our greatest reward is when they are sufficiently convinced as to agree and to appreciate that it is the *right* of all women to choose their own destinies and not to have them dictated by men men who, in fact, have been the architects of the social and religious framework within which they live.

The children are then invited to continue their treatment and we find that they come with the blessings of their mothers who can now relate more sensibly to their children's reaction once counselling commences and follow-up treatment is prescribed. This method has proved highly successful and is recommended for all who have to deal with cases in this category.

# 6. Attitudes towards female circumcision

## Pilot study

A small pilot study, involving 135 individuals (120 women, 15 men) drawn from the majority of the ethnic groups in Sierra Leone, was undertaken to assess attitudes towards female circumcision. The responses recorded cannot be considered as reflecting the attitude of each ethnic group from which representatives were selected, but useful inferences for a broader study can be deducted from this small sample.

## Methodology

The study was carried out at a small clinic in the central part of Freetown, and at the Headquarters of the Planned Parenthood Association, also in Freetown. The objectives were: 1) to dissociate female circumcision from its mystical aura; 2) to test the effect of education on the practice; 3) to test the attitudes of those practising circumcision regarding its continuation or eradication; and 4) to discover the attitude of men on the subject. The interviews were conducted in Krio, the lingua franca of Sierra Leone. The respondents represented each ethnic group and mixed groups resident in Freetown at the time of the interview. Ethnic affiliation, occupation, religion, educational level and socio-economic status were all taken into consideration. Interviews were conducted by me, in the form of conversation.

## Results

All 135 were aware of the existence of female circumcision in the community, and that it was linked to the religion and culture of those practising it. The younger, single girls talked freely about it, so did the older women; but the middle-aged women were at first reluctant and shy. One respondent, who still believed in the traditional, mystical taboos, hoped that her mother would not die because she had talked about female circumcision to a non-circumcised person. One respondent wondered why some members of the community do not practice female circumcision; three believed the practice should not be exposed but remain shrouded in mystery. The men were co-operative, but considered that the practice is in the women's domain.

**Effects of literacy and illiteracy**

Those women who were literate and had been circumcised failed to see the rationale of the practice. Twenty-five percent of the women said they were shocked at what happened to them on the day of their circumcision; it was not what they had expected. One respondent suffered severe bleeding, was infected and taken to hospital. Since circumcision she has suffered from dysmenorrhoea, dyspareunia and recurrent urinary tract infection. She said she will not have her daughters circumcised. Another respondent stated that her sexual feelings had diminished. Her exact words were, "Sexual intercourse is not the same again, it seems as if I have lost something." She asked for reconstruction of her genitalia, but had to be told that was impossible.

Five respondents were prospective candidates for the operation; they wondered if a few gifts that will become obsolete in a few years were worth a life with permanent genital mutilations and asexuality.

The semi-illiterate and the illiterate respondents were die-hard traditionalists who had willingly been circumcised and will subject their daughters to the same fate, for an irrational cause despite the damage to their health. With the exception of the illiterates all the male respondents argued that girls should be given a choice as to whether or not they wanted to be circumcised; to deny them this choice, they said, was a violation of human rights. One illiterate male insisted that all women should be circumcised to keep them in their place.

## Attitudes to continuation or eradication

All literate respondents want the practice to be discontinued, as its health hazards, especially at the time of delivery, are one cause of high maternal and infant mortality.

There are no statistics available to facilitate comparisons in infant mortality and maternal morbidity rates between circumcised and uncircumcised women. Kandeh gives the following infant mortality rates (per 1,000 live births/year) as: Western Area 170; Southern Province 270; Northern Province 238; Eastern Province 247. This strongly indicates that the highest mortality occurs in areas where female circumcision is practiced, although other factors, such as malnutrition, may also contribute. As a result of this high mortality, circumcised women tend to have a large number of children to compensate for those who may die during the first year of life.

Both male and female illiterate respondents want the practice to continue. They argued that if female circumcision is eradicated, part of their culture would likewise be eradicated leaving society bereft of purpose and with nothing to look forward to. They asked what would happen to those who depend on the ceremony fees for subsistence? Some Headwomen are old and cannot do any other work. Younger circumcisers, like the TBAs, Nurse/Midwives and MCH Aids, use their fees to subsidize their meagre salary. Eradication therefore, would bring financial misery to some sections of the community. One illiterate woman respondent adamantly opposed eradication as she feared that the sense of solidarity sustained by the practice would be lost, thus arousing feelings of inequality which may lead to jealously, hatred, disharmony and constant conflict within the community.

35

**Males' attitudes**
Of the 15 males interviewed 10 prefer uncircumcised females as sexual partners, as they have more sexual feelings and share the sexual act and enjoyment with their partners. The remaining (five) males preferred circumcised women; one who had not had sexual intercourse with an uncircumcised woman believed that women are not intended to enjoy sexual intercourse, but their duty was to procreate and be good, docile, obedient housewives.

**Marriage and female circumcision**
Educated men from ethnic groups which traditionally practice circumcision of women insist that, in order to be acceptable to their husbands' community, their wives must be circumcised. In urban areas, however, most men will now marry uncircumcised women as marriage is a matter for the individuals concerned and no longer prearranged by their families; in rural areas marriages are still prearranged.

Illiterate respondents said they would not allow their male relatives or wards to marry uncircumcised women, because, they said, such women are unclean and oversexed.

All the women in the sample said they would not marry an uncircumcised man.

**Health of the initiates**
The ten Krio Christian (uncircumcised) respondents suggested that girls going for circumcision should be medically examined to see if they are physically fit for the ordeal. Those at risk (sicklers, blood dyscrasias, heart diseases, chronic malnutrition etc.) should be excused on the grounds of ill-health. Some respondents were indignant at the way parents dragged their daughters to the Bundo Bush, simply because they feared ostracization by their community. They also suggested that the functions of the clitoris, labiae minora and majora should be explained to those practising circumcision in the hope that such knowledge would encourage minimal mutilation. All the illiterate respondents attributed the health problems attendant upon circumcision to witchcraft, supernatural powers and general bad luck; circumcision, they believed, is a panacea for all illnesses.

# 7. Sexuality and circumcision

## General

Sexuality is the characteristic that bestows upon an individual an understanding of her/himself as a sexual being and enables him/her to develop a successful sexual relationship with other individuals.

It may be more specifically explained as the character of maleness or femaleness. There are two phases to this character: *first* is the way an individual thinks of himself/herself; that is, his/her personal gender role; *second* is the way society regards him/her, that is his/her *social gender role*. The social gender role involves the development of the individual's character to the extent that he/she regards himself/herself as a sexual being operating within the society in which he/she lives.

*Origins of consciousness of human sexuality.* Scientific interest in human sexuality began in the 1960s when physicians became aware of the need for better ways of understanding and managing their patients' sex-related problems. Clinical information was needed in order that the broad array of sexually related problems could be dealt with more effectively. Sexual self-awareness provides the basis for anticipation, stimulation and, ultimately, response in all sexual activity.

The principal pioneers in the field of sexuality — Masters and Johnson of the USA — studied several elements of sexuality and identified four phases: excitement, plateau, orgasm, and resolution. The element of response has been given great prominence since the original work of these researchers. It is now generally believed that true and complete sexual fulfilment can result only from the experience of all stages of sexual response.

In African communities the issue of sexual fulfilment has remained unimportant for centuries. Early societies in Africa established strong controls over the sexual behaviour of their women and devised the brutal means of circumcision to curb female sexual desire and response. The removal of the organ responsible for sexual stimulation (the clitoris) was vital in the fixation of certain values within the community, and to ensure the acceptance of rigid standards of conduct. With the improvement in women's education in Africa and the massive migration from rural areas into the cities, African women have been exposed to an unprecedented extent to a new thinking of female sex roles, fulfilment, and independence and security. Through the continuing flood of information in print, on radio and television, an awareness of the importance of sexual life has been created amongst women who have been taught to disregard this aspect of their lives. Women are, therefore, more ready now than ever before to learn about themselves and to reassess their position in sexual partnership with their menfolk. The traditional views on sexual matters have by no means disappeared. Even with the growing awareness in the modern urban areas of African countries of the importance of sexuality, there have been serious obstacles to effecting the psychological and social transformation required for the attainment of a joyful and purposeful life. In rural areas where most of the people live, and where tradition is linked with spirituality, still greater barriers have to be removed before all women in the region can have an adequate quality of life.

## African traditional concepts of sexuality

Sexuality in the traditional African context differs from the understanding of sexuality in a Western context. There is no known research on African sexuality, consequently the methods currently used to solve sex-related symptoms in African patients are based on Western theories of sexuality.

African traditional lifestyles tend to suppress the *personal* gender role of the individual, whilst enhancing the *social* gender role. This emphasis arises out of the African custom of communal living, and belief in the unity of the extended family.

Traditional sexual relationships occur within a predominantly polygamous family structure. It is difficult to conceive of a relationship, however loose, which will not be interpreted as the making of a family. The boyfriend and girlfriend category, as it is known in Western societies, has no parallel in traditional African society.

A relationship involving sexual intercourse is generally acceptable only between husband and wife/wives. In some African societies, however, particularly those in which a high bride-price means prolonged courtship, pre-marital intercourse, usually resulting in offspring, is neither uncommon nor socially disapproved of. Such a relationship is accepted on the assumption that once the bride-price has been paid the marriage ceremony will take place.

In a polygamous family structure, the husband is the head of the household and is allowed more than one wife. Love and appreciation of man and woman for each other do exist but are suppressed in public; it is unAfrican to display one's feelings in public, the community disapproves of such display. It is believed that emotional feelings between husband and wife/wives is a private matter and that under no circumstances should a wife attempt to exploit or provoke emotional situations to her advantage.

Almost all African societies are patriarchal, and within such a social structure masculine pride dictates that no sign of "softness" or weakness is to be displayed before women. Additionally, sexuality is regarded as a gift, to be used for the procreation of the human species, and any public display of sex-related feeling is seen as debasing this gift.

In some communities, as has been noted, a token expression of the sexual self is permitted: nose-to-nose touching among the Masai in Kenya, and caressing of hands while dancing, is common amongst some West African groups. In many traditional ceremonies, however, the sexes are separated, thus reducing social contact between men and women in public. This traditional separation in public means that sex-related communications may be conveyed only by subtle, covert means.

In some African communities, games, which concentrate on certain masculine attributes, are a device designed to attract the attention of women; for example, spear-throwing, bare-handed fights with animals, wrestling, drum-beating, and dancing. There is never any direct participation by women in these demonstrations of masculinity which serve to establish levels of maleness amongst the protagonists — nevertheless, oral transmission within the group ensures that the women are aware of the prowess of individual men and are thus indirectly involved. In some groups an interest in community affairs, oratory, good-neighbourliness and courtesy are the mens' vehicles for communicating sexual interest in and inclinations towards particular women in the community.

## Sexual reactions in post-circumcised females

To a greater or lesser degree female sexuality is affected by the type of circumcision undergone. Tables 7.1 and 7.2 present the results of interviews with women in Freetown over a 10-month period. Of the 140 women involved 47 were Krio Muslims (Table 7.1) — the only group to practice clitoridectomy — and 93 were from other ethnic groups (Table 7.2) all of which practice excision.

The questions put to all these women concerned:

1) their own levels of consciousness of themselves as sexual beings;
2) their reactions to men's sexual advances;
3) the level of sexual stimulation experienced;
4) the nature of their sexual response;

before (where applicable) and after circumcision. The interviewees' responses were categorized on a 0 to 2 scale (see Tables for interpretation of scale).

## Conclusions

It can be seen that all respondents were proud of their feminine being and personality. This is a reflection of the culture of most communities which support the image of the female as a mother figure existing to reproduce the species and ensure continuity of the community. Many women enjoy the adulation they receive from men at ceremonies and are aware of those outward feminine features which attract the opposite sex. Some communities will go a long way to accentuate such features by moulding them into the desirable form, or by colourful decorations using special beads, or oils and paints.

It is also clear that those who had not engaged in sexual intercourse before circumcision seem not to have experienced any reaction to male advances. This may be as a result of the womanhood training given in the secret societies which possibly conditioned girls to the extent that they subconciously suppress any feelings that may develop during a male's advances. Apparently this psychological barrier remains even after the circumcised female has had sexual experience.

Table 7.1
Clitoridectomy (Krio Muslims)*

| Question type | Response category | Sexual experience | |
|---|---|---|---|
| | | Group 1 pre-circumcision (i.e. sex before circumcision) | Group 2 post-circumcision (i.e. sex after circumcision) |
| 1. | 0 | 0 | 0 |
| | 1 | 0 | 0 |
| | 2 | 14 | 33 |
| 2. | 0 | 4 | 33 |
| | 1 | 0 | 0 |
| | 2 | 10 | 0 |
| 3. | 0 | 3 | 18 |
| | 1 | 11 | 15 |
| | 2 | 0 | 0 |
| 4. | 0 | 3 | 33 |
| | 1 | 11 | 0 |
| | 2 | 0 | 0 |

Key: Question 1:  0 = not conscious         Questions 3:  0 = neutral
                  1 = partly conscious                     1 = mild
                  2 = fully conscious                      2 = intense

     Question 2:  0 = neutral               Question 4:  0 = neutral
                  1 = negative                            1 = excited
                  2 = positive                            2 = orgasm

* No rural women in this group.

The majority of those respondents with sexual experience before circumcision were able to detect personal sexual reactions to male advances both before and after circumcision, the secret society training apparently not producing the same psychological effect on this group as it had on the other.

Furthermore, the tables indicate that of those women with post-circumcision sexual experience who had undergone clitoridectomy about 50% experience only some mild form of sexual stimulation during the sexual act, while for women who had undergone excision this percentage is reduced to 30% for urban women and 12% for rural women. The remaining women with post-circumcision sexual experience reported only neutral or imperceptible stimulation during the sexual act. In the case of women with pre-circumcision sexual experience 79% who had undergone clitoridectomy and 72% of the excised urban women reported mild sexual stimulation during the sexual act.

In general it can be seen that more respondents with pre-circumcision sexual experience (Group 1) were aware of any perceptible sexual stimulation than respondents with post-circumcision (Group 2) sexual experience. No respondents, however, felt any intense stimulation. The difference between the two groups in respect of the numbers of respondents experiencing mild stimulation was unexpected. The reason for this surprising disparity may lie in the fact that respondents in Group 2 lacked any previous sexual experience and were thus unable to make the necessary comparison in order to quantify degrees of stimulation. In short, possibly they were unable to identify what it was they did or did not experience.

Table 7.2
Excision (all ethnic groups except Krio Muslims)

| Question type | Response category* | Sexual experience | | | |
|---|---|---|---|---|---|
| | | Group 1 Pre-circumcision (before circumcision) | | Group 2 Post-circumcision (after circumcision) | |
| | | Rural | Urban | Rural | Urban |
| | | A | B | A | B |
| 1. | 0 | — | 0 | 0 | 0 |
| | 1 | — | 0 | 0 | 0 |
| | 2 | — | 29 | 41 | 23 |
| 2. | 0 | — | 11 | 41 | 23 |
| | 1 | — | 0 | 0 | 0 |
| | 2 | — | 18 | 0 | 0 |
| 3. | 0 | — | 8 | 36 | 16 |
| | 1 | — | 21 | 5 | 7 |
| | 2 | — | 0 | 0 | 0 |
| 4. | 0 | — | 8 | 41 | 23 |
| | 1 | — | 21 | 0 | 0 |
| | 2 | — | 0 | 0 | 0 |

* For key see Table 7.1

The difference between the numbers of those experiencing mild stimulation in Group 1 is small and not as pronounced as expected. It is possible, though as yet unconfirmed, that some degree of sensitivity could have been transferred from the clitoris and labia minora to other parts of the genitalia, and this maybe responsible for the limited overall stimulation felt by those who had been excised.

For Group 2 it is noted that far fewer rural than urban excised women experienced any form of mild stimulation. Again, there may be problems of interpretation and experience, but there is a greater difference in this group between the excised respondents and those who had undergone clitoridectomy. Deterioration in genital sensitivity after excision is clearly more marked than it is in the case of clitoridectomy.

The indication is that for all ethnic groups pre-circumcision sexual experience (Group 1) seems to confer an advantage in relation to sexual pleasure, while none of the respondents with post-circumcision experience only (Group 2) could identify any sexual excitation. Most of those who had had pre-circumcision sexual experience could describe their reactions as being at "the excited" level, but nowhere near the crest of any orgasmic feeling. During the interview women in this group expressed their disappointment with the condition of their womanhood and the diminished level at which they are expected to perform as human beings, despite their inherent qualities which could afford them a fuller, more positive life, and a better, more satisfying relationship with the opposite sex.

Quite a number of women, however, especially those from the rural areas with post-circumcision sexual experience, appeared at their interviews to have resigned themselves to the fate which their society had decreed for them. They felt compelled to abide by the standards of sexuality set by the community and to promote feminine pride and respectability through compliance.

# Appendix 1:

**Results of a survey of 300 women in the Western Area of Sierra Leone: to identify the prevalence of female circumcision and consequent health hazards (January 1985)**

## Introduction and acknowledgements

This study, the first of its kind in Sierra Leone, was confined to the Western Area (see Maps pp. xiv to xvi ), an administrative section of the country in which the capital city Freetown — the destination of rural migrants from all over the country — is situated. Its population is, therefore, reasonably representative of all ethnic groups in Sierra Leone.

The main objectives of the study were:
a) to obtain information about female circumcision (FC) and its effects on the health of women and young girls;
b) to use this information to sensitize both those already circumcised, and potential candidates for circumcision, on the negative effects of the practice.
c) to increase public awareness of the health hazards consequent upon FC.

This research was made possible by the financial, moral and general support from the Population Crisis Committee (PCC) of Washington DC, and the Development Services International (DSI) of Canada. I wish to express my thanks to these organizations for their interest and concern.

I also wish particularly to thank Dr Gordon Wallace for her encouragement, and through her, the staff at the PCC for their technical advice during the conduct of the research.

The statistical analysis of the data was carried out with the help of Techsult Computer Centre; advice on methodology and tabulations of the results was received from Mr Josephus Williams and Dr S.E. Horton, both of whom gave generously of their time to assist us.

In the past it was difficult to obtain information from persons associated with the practice of female circumcision owing to the oaths of secrecy administered at initiation. Thus, concerned individuals, both health professionals and others, have been unable to gain access to circumcised women willing to co-operate to bring about desired change.

Recent contacts with leaders of some secret societies have gradually reduced suspicion between the initiated and sympathetic non-initiates. Many members of these societies have, for the first time, been willing to answer questions on the practice and to venture opinions on social and family attitudes towards potential eradication.

## Methodology

Information was obtained by means of a questionnaire (see pp. 62–66) designed by the Project Director, and consisting of four sections as follows:

Section A: nine questions devoted to socio-demographic information, including two questions on the respondent's husband;
Section B: three questions devoted to the respondent's fertility;
Section C: comprising 17 questions, probed the respondent's opinion on FC. This was the most vital section of the questionnaire in that it examined the reasons for performing FC; whether it should be modified or stopped; the respondent's opinion about the effect of circumcision on her health, and marital relationship; immediate and long-term health problems experienced, and if the respondent would subject her daughters to circumcision.
Section D: was devoted to the confirmation of data collected in Section C by objective observations and pelvic and genital examinations by the medical personnel who conducted the interview.

The research group consisted of two medical officers and eight nurse-midwives. Three teams, with their own headquarters, each surveyed one third of the total area.

### Selection of sample

Three hundred women out of a total population in the Western Area of 500,000 were interviewed. As the services of a professional statistician had not been budgeted for, the sample was not strictly scientific; respondents were selected on a convenience basis of patients attending the family planning and maternity service centres. Data were collected at the following locations:

Planned Parenthood Association Headquarters, Freetown.
Planned Parenthood Association Satellite Clinics scattered over the Greater Freetown area.
The Military Hospital, Wilberforce; and Fourah Bay College Clinic of Mount Aureol. (The catchment area of these clinics includes the mountain villages.)
The Health Centre, Lumley, in the west of Greater Freetown.
Netlands Nursing Home, and Brooklands Maternity Centre (both private institutions) in the west of the inner city area.
The Programme Director's Private Clinic.

## Results and discussion

The survey reveals that the Temne (21 percent) is the largest ethnic group, followed by the Mende (19.3 percent), Limba (13 percent) and Creole (10 percent). A detailed analysis of the 1985 national census is not yet available but the analysis of the 1974 census showed that the Temne and Mende were the largest ethnic groups in the country, thus, the ethnic representation of the survey accords with census findings. The census also shows that even though there is the largest concentration of Krios in the Western Area, the Temne, Mende and Limba, respectively, comprise the numerically largest population groups. In respect of religious affiliation, Muslims form the largest group in the sample — again, this predominance is borne out by official estimates. Regarding educational levels, the study sample diverges from the findings of the national pattern. This is because although there is a predominance of uneducated individuals in the Western Area, there is a higher concentration of educational establishments in Greater Freetown and this fact skewed these figures.

Despite the belief that in Freetown affiliation to traditional practices has been diluted by Westernization it was discovered that almost 90 percent of women had been circumcised. It is also important to note that the practice transcends ethnic divisions; all groups perform FC.

The Tables that follow present the final results of the survey and provide a clear picture of our findings.

**Republic of Sierra Leone**
**National Population Census 1985**

| Administrative Divisions | Total population | Male | Female | Female population as a % of total population |
|---|---|---|---|---|
| Northern Province | 1,262,226 | 604,780 | 657,446 | 37.1 |
| Eastern Province | 960,551 | 492,072 | 468,479 | 26.4 |
| Southern Province | 740,510 | 360,742 | 379,768 | 21.4 |
| Western Area | 554,243 | 287,234 | 267,009 | 15.1 |
| *Total* | | | *1,772,702* | *100.0* |

**Table 1**
**Reasons why female circumcision is performed**

| Rank | Reason | No. of respondents | Percentage of sample |
|------|--------|--------------------|----------------------|
| 1. | Tradition | 257 | 85.67% |
| 2. | Social identity (To belong to the group) | 105 | 35% |
| 3. | Religion | 51 | 17% |
| 4. | Marriage (To increase matrimonial chances) | 12 | 4% |
| 5. | Chastity (Preservation of virginity) | 11 | 3.7% |
| 6. | Female hygiene | 10 | 3.3% |
| 7. | Prevention of promiscuity | 6 | 2% |
| 8. | Fertility enhancement | 3 | 1% |
| 9. | To please husband | 2 | 0.7% |
| 10. | To maintain good health | 1 | 0.3% |

As Table 1 demonstrates, the overriding motivating factor for undergoing female circumcision is tradition (approximately 86 percent of the sample) followed by social identity (35 percent), and religious considerations (17 percent). Social identity is intrinsic to traditional beliefs and in that sense predictable as the second most important factor influencing the practice of FC. That religious considerations were third was surprising in a sample largely comprising city dwellers.

**Table 2**
**Female circumcision according to religious affiliation**

**(Numbers in parentheses are expected frequencies) (Total sample 300)**

| Category | Muslims No. | % | Protestants No. | % | Catholics No. | % | Others No. | % | Total No. | % |
|----------|-------------|-----|-----------------|------|---------------|------|------------|-----|-----------|------|
| Circumcised | 149(135) | 99.3 | 73(88) | 76.8 | 35(36) | 87.5 | 12(11) | 100 | 269 | 89.7 |
| Uncircumcised | 1(15) | 0.7 | 25(10) | 23.2 | 5(4) | 12.5 | 0(1) | 0 | 31 | 10.3 |
| Total | 150 | 100 | 98 | 100 | 40 | 100 | 12 | 100 | 300 | 100 |

$\chi^2 = 40.95$ Highly significant even at 0.001% level

Table 2 provides a breakdown of circumcised and uncircumcised women according to religious affiliation. The results show that out of 150 Muslims interviewed 149 (99.3 percent) were circumcised — a higher figure than expected (135); and of the 40 Roman Catholics interviewed 35 were circumcised, close to the figure expected (36). The total number of Christians (Protestants and Catholics) circumcised was 108, a lower overall figure than was expected (126).

These figures are, however, not conclusive — a much larger, random sample may have clarified the position. Although most Sierra Leonians are Muslim, Catholicism is a very active evangelizing and converting force. It is possible that many women were circumcised prior to conversion to Catholicism.

**Table 3**
**FC according to ethnic group (numbers in parentheses are expected frequencies)**
**(Total sample 300)**

| Ethnic group | Numbers | | | Percentage | | |
|---|---|---|---|---|---|---|
| | Circum-cised | Uncircum-cised | Total | Circum-cised | Uncircum-cised | Total |
| Temne | 65(56) | 0(7) | 63 | 100 | 0 | 100 |
| Mende | 56(52) | 2(6) | 58 | 96.6 | 3.4 | 100 |
| Limba | 39(35) | 0(4) | 39 | 100 | 0 | 100 |
| Krio | 13(27) | 17(3) | 30 | 42.3 | 56.7 | 100 |
| Lokko | 26(23) | 0(3) | 26 | 100 | 0 | 100 |
| Foulah | 16(14) | 0(2) | 16 | 100 | 0 | 100 |
| Susu | 11(11) | 1(1) | 12 | 91.7 | 8.3 | 100 |
| Mandingo | 10(9) | 0(1) | 10 | 100 | 0 | 100 |
| Kono | 10(9) | 0(1) | 10 | 100 | 0 | 100 |
| Yalunka | 5(4) | 0(1) | 5 | 100 | 0 | 100 |
| Kroo | 3(—) | 1(—) | 4 | 75 | 25 | 100 |
| Other | 17(24) | 10(3) | 27 | 63 | 37 | 100 |
| *Total* | *269* | *31* | *300* | *89.7* | *10.3* | *100* |

For absolute numbers $\chi^2 = 114.385$ highly significant even at 0.0001%.

Table 3 illustrates the importance of tradition in influencing the practice of FC. All Temne, Limba, Lokko and Foulah women in the sample were circumcised, and 56 out of 58 Mende women. The expected numbers — with the exception of that for Krio women — were generally lower than the actual numbers. From which we may, perhaps, speculate that tradition is a less strong influence amongst the Krio.

**Table 4**
**Circumcised/uncircumcised according to educational level (Numbers in parentheses are expected frequencies) (Total sample 300)**

| | Numbers | | | Percentage | | |
|---|---|---|---|---|---|---|
| | Circum-cised | Uncircum-cised | Total | Circum-cised | Uncircum-cised | Total |
| No education | 104 (93) | 0 (11) | 104 | 100 | 0 | 100 |
| Primary | 45 (45) | 4 (4) | 49 | 90 | 10 | 100 |
| Secondary | 95 (105) | 22 (12) | 117 | 81.2 | 18.8 | 100 |
| Tertiary | 24 (26) | 5 (3) | 29 | 82.8 | 17.2 | 100 |
| Professional | 1 (1) | — (0) | 1 | 100 | 0 | 100 |
| *Total* | *269* | *31* | *300* | *89.7* | *10.3* | *100* |

$\chi^2 = 23.073$: Highly significant even at 0.001% level

Education by, presumably, neutralizing traditional beliefs and practices, may be expected to reduce the number of those circumcised. Table 4, however, suggests that there are other, overriding factors influencing submission to the practice. Clearly, no valid inferences can be made from the one professional woman in the sample, or from the small tertiary sample. One important factor is that induction into a secret society usually occurs at an early age — for example, before a candidate's tenth birthday.

The following Tables: 5A, 5B, 5C and 5D, provide data on age at circumcision by: ethnic group, occupation, educational level, and religious affiliation respectively.

Table 5A indicates that, generally, most girls were circumcised before the age of 16 years — that is, before they were sufficiently mature to make their own decisions or before other, external influences had been in operation. Certainly, circumcision preceded marriage, and the model age is early puberty.

Of the 300 respondents the earliest age for circumcision was seven years. The oldest was 30 years, and was represented by one respondent. Probably she had undergone clitoridectomy at an earlier age, but at 30 years she underwent excision in order to advance to the rank of *Digba/Sowie* in her society.

Table 5B indicates that by the onset of puberty (12 years) almost 66 percent of respondents had been circumcised, and by 15 years 90 percent. Interestingly, almost 75 percent were housewives or business women — occupations that require very little formal education.

Table 5C shows that almost 40 percent of initiates were illiterate; and that over 50 percent did not advance beyond primary school. To account for the 75 percent comprising housewives and business women in Table 5B, a greater number of those educated to secondary level must be included. This pattern differs little from that of Sierra Leonian women in general, even among non-society members practicing FC. The one post-graduate/professional women undertook to be initiated at an age when she could and did take the decision herself and, as she stated at the interview, paid her own expenses. Perhaps, like Gandhi exchanging his Western suit for a dhoti, she was making a deliberate gesture in favour of the values of preserving tradition.

Table 5D suggests that although some religions may not positively encourage FC neither do they positively discourage the practice, possibly perceiving some beneficial results. Interestingly, 10 women (5 Protestant, 2 Catholic, 3 Muslim) were circumcised at an age when it is to be assumed they were able to take their own decisions.

**Table 5A**
**Age at circumcision by ethnic group**

| | 5–10 No. | 5–10 % | 11–13 No. | 11–13 % | 14–16 No. | 14–16 % | 17–19 No. | 17–19 % | 20–30 No. | 20–30 % | Total: 5–30 years No. | Total: 5–30 years % |
|---|---|---|---|---|---|---|---|---|---|---|---|---|
| Temne | 26 | 41.27 | 14 | 22.22 | 20 | 31.75 | 2 | 3.17 | 1 | 1.59 | 63 | 100 |
| Mende | 20 | 35.71 | 10 | 17.86 | 13 | 23.21 | 7 | 12.5 | 6 | 10.71 | 56 | 99.99 |
| Limba | 14 | 35.90 | 14 | 35.90 | 9 | 23.07 | 2 | 5.13 | 0 | 0 | 39 | 100 |
| Krio | 2 | 15.38 | 1 | 7.69 | 9 | 69.23 | 0 | 0 | 1 | 7.69 | 13 | 99.99 |
| Lokko | 16 | 61.54 | 7 | 24.92 | 2 | 7.79 | 1 | 3.85 | 0 | 0 | 26 | 100 |
| Foulah | 9 | 56.25 | 5 | 31.25 | 0 | 0 | 0 | 0 | 2 | 12.50 | 16 | 100 |
| Susu | 5 | 45.45 | 1 | 9.09 | 4 | 36.36 | 1 | 9.09 | 0 | 0 | 11 | 100 |
| Mandingo | 3 | 30 | 3 | 30 | 4 | 40 | 0 | 0 | 0 | 0 | 10 | 100 |
| Kono | 5 | 50 | 4 | 40 | 1 | 10 | 0 | 0 | 0 | 0 | 10 | 100 |
| Yalunka | 1 | 20 | 2 | 40 | 2 | 40 | 0 | 0 | 0 | 0 | 5 | 100 |
| Kroo | 2 | 66.1 | 0 | 0 | 1 | 33.3 | 0 | 0 | 0 | 0 | 3 | 100 |
| Other | 7 | 41.18 | 5 | 29.41 | 4 | 23.53 | 1 | 5.88 | 0 | 0 | 17 | 100 |
| *Total* | *110* | *40.89* | *66* | *24.54* | *69* | *25.65* | *14* | *5.20* | *10* | *3.72* | *269* | *100* |

**Table 5B**
**Age at circumcision by occupation (Total sample 269)**

| Age | Housewife | | Business Women | | Student | | Professional | | Unemployed including unmarried | | Total | |
|---|---|---|---|---|---|---|---|---|---|---|---|---|
| | No. | % | No. | % | No. | % | No. | % | No. | % | No. | % |
| 5–9 | 36 | 13.38 | 55 | 20.45 | 10 | 3.72 | 6 | 2.23 | 3 | 1.12 | 110 | 40.89 |
| 10–12 | 24 | 8.92 | 28 | 10.41 | 8 | 2.97 | 4 | 1.49 | 2 | 0.74 | 66 | 24.53 |
| 13–15 | 19 | 2.06 | 26 | 9.67 | 9 | 3.35 | 13 | 4.83 | 2 | 0.74 | 69 | 25.65 |
| 16–19 | 7 | 2.60 | 2 | 0.74 | 3 | 1.12 | 2 | 0.74 | — | 0 | 14 | 5.20 |
| 20–30 | 3 | 1.12 | 1 | 0.37 | 3 | 1.12 | 2 | 1.12 | — | 0 | 10 | 3.72 |
| Total | 89 | 33.09 | 112 | 41.64 | 33 | 12.27 | 28 | 10.41 | 7 | 2.60 | 269 | 100 |

**Table 5C**
**Age at circumcision by educational level**

| Age | Primary | | Secondary | | Tertiary College or University | | Post-Graduate/ Professional | | Illiterate | | Total | |
|---|---|---|---|---|---|---|---|---|---|---|---|---|
| | No. | % | No. | % | No. | % | No. | % | No. | % | No. | % |
| 5–9 | 22 | 8.15 | 35 | 13.01 | 5 | 1.86 | 0 | — | 48 | 17.84 | 110 | 40.89 |
| 10–13 | 9 | 3.35 | 18 | 6.69 | 4 | 1.49 | 0 | — | 35 | 13.01 | 66 | 24.54 |
| 14–16 | 12 | 4.46 | 29 | 10.78 | 11 | 4.09 | 0 | — | 17 | 6.32 | 69 | 25.64 |
| 17–19 | 2 | 0.74 | 9 | 3.35 | 1 | 0.37 | 0 | — | 2 | 0.74 | 14 | 5.20 |
| 20–30 | 0 | — | 4 | 1.49 | 3 | 1.12 | 1 | 0.37 | 2 | 0.74 | 10 | 3.72 |
| All ages | 45 | 16.73 | 95 | 35.32 | 24 | 8.92 | 1 | 0.37 | 104 | 38.66 | 269 | 100 |

**Table 5D**
**Age at circumcision by religious affiliation**

| Age | Protestants | | Catholics | | Muslims | | Others | | Total | |
|---|---|---|---|---|---|---|---|---|---|---|
| | *No.* | *%* | *No.* | *%* | *No.* | *%* | *No.* | *%* | *No.* | *%* |
| 5–9 | 9 | 3.35 | 35 | 13.01 | 64 | 23.79 | 2 | 0.74 | 110 | 40.89 |
| 10–12 | 7 | 2.60 | 16 | 5.95 | 35 | 13.01 | 8 | 2.97 | 66 | 24.54 |
| 13–15 | 8 | 2.97 | 15 | 1.86 | 44 | 1.21 | 0 | 0.74 | 69 | 25.65 |
| 16–19 | 6 | 2.23 | 5 | 1.66 | 3 | 1.12 | 0 | — | 14 | 5.20 |
| 20–30 | 5 | 1.86 | 2 | 0.74 | 3 | 1.12 | 0 | 0 | 10 | 3.72 |
| All ages | 35 | 13.01 | 73 | 27.14 | 149 | 55.39 | 12 | 4.46 | 269 | 100 |

**Table 6A**
**Type of FC with instrument used (absolute numbers)**

| Type | Razor blade No. | Traditional knife No. | Surgical scalpel No. | Broken bottle No. | Others No. | Total No. |
|---|---|---|---|---|---|---|
| Type I | 32 | 62 | 2 | 1 | 8 | 105 |
| Type II | 48 | 102 | 4 | 3 | 4 | 161 |
| Type III | 1 | 2 | — | — | — | 3 |
| *Total* | *81* | *166* | *6* | *4* | *12* | *269* |

Table 6A indicates that FC Types I and II are dominant (266 out of the 269 respondents). Type III appears not to form part of traditional practices in Sierra Leone. Instruments most frequently used are traditional knife and razor blades; the surgical scalpel is a recent introduction. As members climb the educational ladder so surgical instruments are introduced.

**Table 6B**
**Instruments used as the principal axis of investigation (percentages)**

| Type | Razor blade % | Traditional knife % | Surgical scalpel % | Broken bottle % | Others % | Total % |
|---|---|---|---|---|---|---|
| Type I | 39.51 | 37.35 | 33.33 | 25 | 66.67 | 39.03 |
| Type II | 59.26 | 61.45 | 66.67 | 75 | 33.33 | 59.85 |
| Type III | 1.23 | 1.20 | 0 | 0 | 0 | 1.12 |
| *Total* | *100* | *100* | *100* | *100* | *100* | *100* |

Table 6B indicates the predominance of Type II circumcision. Apparently the instrument used does not determine the type of FC performed except, perhaps, 'Others' which are mainly used for Type I.

**Table 6C**
**Type of FC as the principal axis of investigation (percentages)**

| Type of FC | Razor blade % | Traditional knife % | Surgical scalpel % | Broken bottle % | Others % | Total % |
|---|---|---|---|---|---|---|
| Type I | 30.48 | 59.05 | 1.90 | 0.95 | 7.62 | 100 |
| Type II | 29.81 | 63.35 | 2.48 | 1.88 | 2.48 | 100 |
| Type III | 33.33 | 66.67 | — | — | — | 100 |
| *Total* | *30.11* | *61.71* | *2.23* | *1.49* | *4.46* | *100* |

Table 6C demonstrates that the dominant instrument used is the traditional knife. Possibly this instrument has some esoteric significance, or its superiority over others has been proved over time, or operators have acquired dexterity in its use.

**Table 7A**
**Type of FC by category of operator (absolute numbers)**
**(Expected numbers in parentheses)**

| Type | Digba/ Sowie/ TBA | Herbalist | Trained midwife | Surgeon | Total |
|------|------|------|------|------|------|
| | No. | No. | No. | No. | No. |
| Type I | 97 (99) | 4 (3) | 4 (3) | 0 (0) | 105 |
| Type II | 155 (152) | 2 (4) | 3 (4) | 1 (1) | 161 |
| Type III | 2 (3) | 1 (0) | 0 (0) | 0 (0) | 3 |
| Total | 254 | 7 | 7 | 1 | 269 |

$\chi^2 = 14.644$

Table 7A shows the dominance of society leaders in the initiation rites (Types I and II, column one) and that they perform more circumcisions Type II than I or III. The presence of a surgeon is innovatory, but as increasing numbers of society members themselves become medically qualified whilst remaining adherents to tradition, this may become more common.

**Table 7B**
**Type of FC as principle axis of investigation (in percentages)**

| Type of FC | Digba/ Sowie/ TBA | Herbalist | Trained midwife | Surgeon | Total |
|------|------|------|------|------|------|
| | % | % | % | % | % |
| Type I | 92.38 | 3.81 | 3.81 | 0 | 100 |
| Type II | 96.27 | 1.24 | 1.86 | 0.63 | 100 |
| Type III | 66.67 | 33.33 | 0 | 0 | 100 |
| Total | 94.42 | 2.60 | 2.60 | 0.38 | 100 |

The above table shows predominant types of FC performed. Again, the pre-eminence of the societies' leaders in the rites is demonstrated.

Table 8A indicates that pain is experienced irrespective of the type of circumcision.
    Tables 8B, 8C and 8D are reproduced for interest, but what they show cannot be considered significant because: 1) the term 'shock' (an assemblage of symptoms) was not clearly understood by interviewers (Table 8B); 2) less than 10 percent for Type I, and 20 percent for Type II and none for Type III experienced urine retention; and 3) the presence or absence of haemorrhage is not dependent on the type of FC performed.

**Table 8A**
**Incidence of pain (total sample 269)**

| Circumcision Type | Observed Yes | | No |
|---|---|---|---|
| I | 98 (101) | 7 (4) | 105 |
| II | 159 (156) | 2 (5) | 161 |
| III | 3 (3) | 0 (0) | 3 |
| *Total* | *260* | *9* | *269* |

$\chi^2 = 5.887$

**Table 8B**
**Incidence of shock (Total sample 269)**

| Circumcision Type | Observed Yes | No | Total |
|---|---|---|---|
| I | 19 (14) | 86 (91) | 105 |
| II | 16 (22) | 145 (139) | 161 |
| III | 1 (0) | 2 (3) | 3 |
| *Total* | *36* | *233* | *269* |

$\chi^2 = 4.689$

**Table 8C**
**Incidence of urinary retention (Total sample 269)**

| Circumcision Type | Observed Yes | No | Total |
|---|---|---|---|
| I | 9 (14) | 96 (91) | 105 |
| II | 26 (21) | 135 (140) | 161 |
| III | 0 (0) | 3 (3) | 3 |
| *Total* | *35* | *234* | *269* |

$\chi^2 = 3.678$

**Table 8D**
**Incidence of haemorrhage (Total sample 269)**

| Circumcision FC | Observed Yes | No | Total |
|---|---|---|---|
| I | 58 (54) | 47 (51) | 105 |
| II | 79 (83) | 82 (78) | 161 |
| III | 2 (2) | 1 (1) | 3 |
| *Total* | *139* | *130* | *269* |

$\chi^2 = 1.242$

**Table 8E**
**Keloid scar resulting from immediate complications (Total sample 300)**

|  | Present | Absent | Total |
|---|---|---|---|
|  | 95 | 104 | 199 |
|  | 44 | 57 | 101 |
| Total | 139 | 161 | 300 |

$\chi^2 = 0.4695$ not significant even at 0.05% probability level.

Table 8E shows that for 67% of circumcised women a keloid scar on the vulva results. This may even be a stamp of identification for admission to other branches of the society, and, therefore, may be sought after. It is traditional for youths to mark and scar themselves as a sign of courage and endurance; women's initiation societies also include training in these qualities. Thus they see no disadvantage in being scarred.

The medical profession is distressed by the fact that almost 33% of all circumcised women eventually develop prolapses (Table 9). Of the 32% of circumcised women without any visual sequalae many may have other problems, for example, at childbirth, psychological disturbances, and so on.

**Table 9**
**Visual malformations present by type of circumcision (Total sample 269)**

| Type | Keloid scar | | Fistula | | Prolapse | | Cysts | | Abscesses | | None | |
|---|---|---|---|---|---|---|---|---|---|---|---|---|
|  | No. | % | No. | % | No. | % | No. | % | No. | % | No. | % |
| I | 62 | 59 | 0 | 0 | 32 | 30 | 0 | 0 | 0 | 0 | 22 | 21 |
| II | 104 | 65 | 1 | (0.6) | 49 | 30 | 8 | 5 | 4 | 2.5 | 63 | 39 |
| III | 2 | 67 | 0 | 0 | 1 | 33 | 0 | 0 | 0 | 0 | 1 | 3 |
| Total for all types | 168 | | 1 | | 82 | | 8 | | 4 | | 86 | |

The above Table demonstrates the extent of visual, genital malformations resulting from each of the three types of FC.

## Attitudes Towards Modifying Female Circumcision (FC)
Respondents who favoured modifying FC thought the operation should be made less painful, brutal, or dangerous. Most of these respondents indicated that they would like to see a more sanitary/hygienic area where circumcision was performed; a sterilised instrument for each initiate; local analgesic application to the vulva areas; less force to hold down initiates; the provision of some nurses or paramedicals to attend emergency cases over the initiation period; more first-aid kits to deal with emergency cases; and a more sympathetic hospital staff, including doctors, to attend to their cases when brought to hospitals. Respondents gave personal experiences of circumcisers who have lost the lives of initiates because the doctors on duty at hospitals where they took emergencies were hostile to them and to the initiate.

Educated respondents thought that initiates should be given anti-tetanus injections prior to initiation, as well as a physical examination to exclude those suffering from sickle-cell anaemia or other blood dyscrasias. In effect a "No Opinion" reply indicates that the respondent *at the moment* is not in favour of stopping or modifying FC, and thus reinforces, by default, the status quo, i.e. continuation of FC. "No Opinion" respondents offered further information, or on further consideration, may choose to go either direction. Attitudes toward stopping or modifying FC are significantly affected by religious affiliation.

WHO opposes modification, institutionalization, and modernization of FC.

**Table 10A**
**Attitudes towards modification of FC by those who experienced immediate complications (Total sample 300)**

| Response | Haemor-rhage | Shock | Pain | Total Responses |
|---|---|---|---|---|
| Yes | 67 (72) | 20 (72) | 128 (72) | 215 |
| No | 70 (72) | 16 (72) | 130 (72) | 216 |
| None | 163 (156) | 264 (156) | 42 (156) | 469 |
| *Total* | *300* | *300* | *300* | *900* |

$\chi^2$ with four degrees of freedom = 330.217 which is highly significant even at 0.001% level

**Table 10B**
**Attitudes towards modification of FC by those who experienced visible/permanant problems. (Numbers in parenthesis are expected frequencies by marginal distributions) (Total sample 300)**

| Response | Scars | Menstrual problems | No problems | Total responses |
|---|---|---|---|---|
| Yes | 70 (50) | 27 (50) | 52 (50) | 149 |
| No | 43 (43) | 12 (43) | 75 (43) | 130 |
| None | 187 (207) | 261 (207) | 173 (207) | 621 |
| *Total* | *300* | *300* | *300* | *900* |

$\chi^2$ = 86.18 which is highly significant even at 0.001% level

**Table 10C**
**Attitudes towards modification of FC by those who experienced obstetric complications. (Numbers in parenthesis are expected frequencies) (Total sample 300)**

| Response | Prolonged | Vaginal | Stillbirths | Complica-tions | Total responses |
|---|---|---|---|---|---|
| Yes | 40 (42) | 58 (42) | 18 (42) | 53 (42) | 169 |
| No | 30 (40) | 46 (40) | 13 (40) | 72 (40) | 161 |
| None | 230 (218) | 196 (218) | 269 (218) | 175 (218) | 870 |
| *Total* | *300* | *300* | *300* | *300* | *1200* |

$\chi^2$ = 92.913 which is highly significant even at the 0.001% probability level

**Table 10D**
**Attitudes towards modification of FC according to whether or not daughters are circumcised. (Numbers in parenthesis are expected frequencies) (Total sample 176)**

| Attitude | Daughters circumcised | Daughters uncircumcised | Total responses |
|---|---|---|---|
| | (i) | (ii) | |
| Modify | 23 (34) | 62 (52) | 86 |
| | (iii) | (iv) | |
| Do not modify | 45 (35) | 45 (55) | 90 |
| Total | 69 | 107 | 176 |

The $\chi^2$ of this Table is 9.006 which is significant both at the 0.05 and the 0.01 probability level. Therefore there is a significant association between the attitudes of parents and whether they send their children for FC.

Tables 10A, 10B and 10C show that when respondents realized the problems caused by FC they were generally in favour of some modification of the practice. It remains to identify the means to convince traditional leaders of this; education can perform a vital role in this respect.

## Attitudes Towards Ending Female Circumcision (FC)

After explanation, many women realized for the first time that their gynaecological problems were related to their FC operation several years previously. Many of these were then willing to take the decision not to send their daughters for FC.
Attitudes towards ending FC are significantly affected by:

a) Ethnic group;
b) Religious affiliation: A majority of Protestants favour stopping FC; a majority of Catholics favour continuation. Although a large majority of Muslims favour continuation, a surprising 21% favour its abolition.
c) Level of education: The majority of those favouring continuation of FC are uneducated or have primary education only. Those with secondary education also still favour continuation but by a smaller majority. A vast majority of respondents with college, university or postgraduate education (79%) favour stopping the practice.

Factors which show little effect on attitudes toward stopping FC are post-operative care, age at circumcision, and occupation. Pain, immediate and long-term health complications at circumcision do not influence respondents in favour of stopping FC as endurance of pain is seen as a sign of bravery.

Attitude toward stopping FC influences whether or not a respondent has her daughter circumcised. This proportion was larger than would have been expected in the light of other factors.

57

**Table 11A**
**Attitudes towards ending FC according to whether or not daughters are circumcised.**
**(Numbers in parenthesis are expected frequencies) (Total sample 176)**

| Attitude | Daughters circumcised | Daughters uncircumcised | Total responses |
|---|---|---|---|
| Should be ended | 7 (22) | 49 (34) | 56 |
| Should not be ended | 62 (47) | 58 (73) | 120 |
| Total | 69 | 107 | 176 |

$\chi^2 = 24.5744$ which is highly significant even at 0.001% level

**Table 11B**
**Attitudes towards ending FC according to age at which respondents were circumcised.**
**(Numbers in parenthesis are expected frequencies) (Total sample 269)**

| Response | 5–10 | 11–13 | 14–16 | 17–19 | 20–30 | Total responses |
|---|---|---|---|---|---|---|
| Yes | 34 (33) | 15 (20) | 26 (21) | 4 (4) | 3 (3) | 82 |
| No | 75 (76) | 51 (46) | 45 (49) | 10 (10) | 7 (7) | 188 |
| None | 1 (0) | 0 | 0 | 0 (0) | 0 (0) | 1 |
| Total | 110 | 66 | 71 | 14 | 10 | 271 |

$\chi^2 = 4.672$

**Table 11C**
**Attitudes towards ending FC according to religious affiliation (Numbers in parenthesis are expected frequencies) (Total sample 300)**

| Response | Roman Catholic | Protestant | Muslim | Others | Total responses |
|---|---|---|---|---|---|
| Yes | 15 (14) | 52 (34) | 31 (52) | 6 (4) | 104 |
| No | 24 (25) | 41 (62) | 119 (95) | 6 (8) | 190 |
| None | 1 (1) | 5 (2) | 0 (3) | 0 (0) | 6 |
| Total | 40 | 98 | 150 | 12 | 300 |

$\chi^2 = 40.578$

Tables 11A and 11B should be interpreted together. They show that there is a basis for modification and even ending FC. Tradition is not strong enough to prevent this. Attitudes favouring modification or even ending the practice of FC can be developed among Sierra Leonian women by means of a massive health education scheme at all levels emphasizing the dangerous consequences of the practice.

The similarity between expected and observed figures could be as a result of chance. Table 6A, therefore, does not prove that age at circumcision influences attitude towards ending it.

These figures are highly significant, even at the 0.001 probability level, in that they indicate that religious affiliation does influence the attitude of women towards ending of FC. Action can, therefore, be mounted against the leaders of religion to try to convince them of the foolhardiness of continuing FC in the light of massive evidence proving that it leads to great suffering, as well as mutilation of the body, to preserve whi b is a basic human right. To ensure health for all by the year 2000 in Sierra Leone, the harmful effects of certain traditional practices on the health and wellbeing of our women should be forcefully highlighted to bring to religious leaders the realization that posterity will blame them if by suppressing hard facts they thus enslave our women in the shackles of outmoded and dangerous practices.

# Conclusions and Recommendations

The sample size of this Survey was small, yet it produced many significant facts, notably the extent of mutilation and unnecessary suffering caused by circumcision of women, and the health consequences for the women. The questions and interviews revealed that the most widespread medical problems were:

1. One-third of all respondents suffered prolapses.

2. More than 50% had keloids and scar tissues in the perineal regions and experienced tears during labour.

3. A significant proportion reported prolonged and difficult labour.

4. First pregnancies in circumcised women frequently resulted in stillbirths owing to obstructions during labour.

5. A greater weight of opinion favours modifying the practice rather than stopping it. Respondents identified modification as removal of fewer tissues from the perineal region, improvement of sanitation, use of anaesthetics, etc.

6. A low educational level may be one negative factor to affect efforts to eradicate circumcision of women.

7. Most operations are carried out by the Society leaders (*digbas*, *sowies*, TBAs); women encourage the practice, men pay for the initiation ceremony. In areas where circumcision is traditionally practiced, men will not marry a woman who has not been trained as a member of a Society. It was also revealed that there is probably hidden fear of reprisal against anyone openly condemning what is sanctified by the Society's leaders. Post-operative care was not a consideration for those advocating either modifying or stopping circumcision of women.

8. The Survey also brought out the following sociological aspects:

a) the Society caters for the psycho-social need of women's solidarity over which their husbands have no power;

b) women actively seek membership of circumcision Societies;

c) the Society's rites are firmly rooted in tradition which appears to be particularly strong among those ethnic groups with the highest prevalence of FC, notably the Foulah, Temne, Lokko and Susu;

d) there is evidence that Christians and Krios are gradually being drawn into the Societies in which circumcision is a requirement for membership;

e) the Muslim faith was believed to endorse the practice possibly because of the modifying effect on women's libido, inducing docility, contentment and pliability. It may also be considered important in polygamous households in order to render the women less sexually demanding.

f) the compulsion of tradition means that most parents send their daughters to be circumcised long before they are old enough to make decisions for themselves.

## Recommendations

In view of the serious consequences of circumcision for women, it is recommended that:

1. A countrywide study should be undertaken, involving a much larger sample and structured in such a way as to investigate the various economic levels, regions

and ethnic groups in greater depth. This study should include factors not covered in the present, limited survey.

Such a study might also be expanded to cover West Africa; the findings might then form the basis for WHO action in this region. A standardized questionnaire could be used throughout the area.

2. Materials for health education should be prepared with a view to supporting the work initiated in this wider study in order to sensitize African women to the health consequences of circumcision of females; this could be done concomitantly with the expanded research proposed and materials already in existence —provided by the Inter-African Committee — to be used wherever needed.

3. The ultimate goal should be elimination of female circumcision. In order to maintain the traditional values associated with the practice, however, it might be of value to develop a symbolic substitute, a token ceremony, to confer the psychological benefits derived by African women from membership of a sorority.

4. Efforts to raise the educational level of all African women should be intensified so that with better education, women can be more objective in their judgement of social issues, especially those that affect their health.

# Appendix 2:

# Questionnaire: January 1985

## Identification

Client's Full Name and Address:

## A. Socio-Demographic Information

### A1. Ethnic Group:

| | | | | | |
|---|---|---|---|---|---|
| 1. _____ Temne | 5. ___Foulah | 9. ___Madingo |
| 2. _____ Creole | 6. ___Kono | 10. ___Susu |
| 3. _____ Mende | 7. ___Krio | 11. ___Kissy |
| 4. _____ Limba | 8. ___Lokko | 12. ___Yalunka |
| | | 13. ___Other, specify |

### A2. Religion:

1. _____ Roman Catholic     3. _____ Muslim
2. _____ Protestant          4. _____ Other, specify

### A3. Age:

1. _____ 15–19 yrs          3. _____ 30–39 yrs
2. _____ 20–29 yrs          4. _____ 40 and over

### A4. Marital Status:

1. _____ Single             2. _____ Married
3. _____ Divorced           4. _____ Widowed

### A5. Husband's Occupation:

1. _____ Farmer                      4. _____ Civil Servant
2. _____ Labourer                    5. _____ Professional
3. _____ Trader/Businessman          6. _____ Unemployed

**A6. Husband's Ethnic Group:**

1. _____ Temne    6. ____Kono    11. ____Kissy
2. _____ Creole    7. ____Krio    12. ____Yalunka
3. _____ Mende    8. ____Lokko    13. ____Other, specify
4. _____ Limba    9. ____Madingo
5. _____ Foulah    10. ____Susu

**A7. Client's Occupation:**

1. _____ Housewife    3. _____ Student
2. _____ Trader/Business-    4. _____ Professional
        woman    5. _____ Unemployed

**A8. Type of Marriage:**

1. _____ Polygamous    2. _____ Monogamous

**A9. Level of Education:**

1. _____ Primary    2. _____ Secondary
3. _____ College/University    4. _____ Professional
5. _____ None

# B. Fertility

**B1.** Gravida _____

**B2.** Parity _____

**B3.** No. of children _____

# C. Opinion of Female Circumcision

**C1. Are you a member of the female society**

2. _____ Yes    2. _____ No

**C2. If yes, why is F.C. done?**

1. _____ Tradition    6. _____ To please fiancé/husband
2. _____ Religious demand    7. _____ To belong to the group/or to identify with the group
3. _____ Hygiene    8. _____ To enhance fertility
4. _____ Preservation of virginity    9. _____ To increase matrimonial opportunities
5. _____ Prevention of promiscuity    10. _____ To maintain good health

**C3. Should the practice be modified?**
1. _____ Yes          2. _____ No

**C3A. Should the practice be stopped?**
1. _____ Yes          2. _____ No

**C4. Do you think the practice affects a woman's health?**
1. _____ Yes          2. _____ No
Say why _____

**C5. Do you think the practice affects a woman's marital relationship?**
1. _____ Yes          2. _____ No
If so, how_____

**C6. If circumcised, at what age were you circumcised?** _____

**C7. Who performed the operation?**
1. _____ TBA/Digba          3. _____ Trained midwife
          Sowie
2. _____ Native doctor      4. _____ Doctor

**C8. What instrument was used?**
1. _____ Blade          2. _____ Scalpel
2. _____ Knife          4. _____ Broken bottle
                          5. _____ Other, specify

**C9. Who encouraged the operation?**
1. _____ Mother    3. _____Aunt      5. _____Husband
2. _____ Father    4. _____Fiancé    6. _____Female
                                                  relatives

**C10. Who paid for the operation?**
1. _____ Mother    3. _____Aunt      5. _____Husband
2. _____ Father    4. _____Fiancé    6. _____Female
                                                  relatives

**C11. How did you pay?**
1. _____ Cash          2. _____ Kind/Gifts

**C12. What post-operative care was given?**
1. _____ First-aid      3. _____ Other, specify
2. _____ Herbs          4. _____ None

## C13. What immediate complications were experienced?

| | | | | |
|---|---|---|---|---|
| 1. | _____ | Haemorrhage | 5. _____ | Injury to neighbouring structures |
| 2. | _____ | Shock | 6. _____ | Tetanus |
| 3. | _____ | Infection e.g. fever | 7. _____ | Pain |
| 4. | _____ | Urinary retention | 8. _____ | None |

## C14. What long term complications?

| | | | | |
|---|---|---|---|---|
| 1. | _____ | Scars, and keloid | 5. _____ | Chronic pelvic infection |
| 2. | _____ | Cysts | 6. _____ | Menstrual problems |
| 3. | _____ | Abscess | 7. _____ | None |
| 4. | _____ | Urine retention/ urinary tract infection | | |

## C15. What complications at marriage/childbirth

| | | | | |
|---|---|---|---|---|
| 1. | _____ | Dyspareunia | 6. _____ | Cystoceles |
| 2. | _____ | Frigidity | 7. _____ | Tears – Vaginal/ Rectal |
| 3. | _____ | Infertility due to infection | 8. _____ | Still births |
| 4. | _____ | Prolonged/ obstructed labour | 9. _____ | Urinary infection |
| 5. | _____ | Fistulae – Urinary/ Rectal | 10. _____ | None |

## C16. What other complications?

| | | | | |
|---|---|---|---|---|
| 1. | _____ | Anxiety | 4. _____ | Sense of inadequacy |
| 2. | _____ | Depression | 5. _____ | None |
| 3. | _____ | Psychosis | | |

## C17. Do you have any daughters?

| | | | |
|---|---|---|---|
| 1. | _____ Yes | 2. | _____ No |

If yes, are any circumcised?

| | | | |
|---|---|---|---|
| 1. | _____ Yes | 2. | _____ No |

Explain why_____

# D. Report on examination by MO/Nurse/Midwife

## D1. Has F.C. been performed?

| | | | |
|---|---|---|---|
| 1. | _____ Yes | 2. | _____ No |

## D1A.  If yes, state which type?

1. _____ Clitoridectomy      3. _____ Excision
2. _____ Infibulation

## D2.  State any visual malformation observed:

1. _____ Keloid scar      3. _____ Abscess
2. _____ Cysts          4. _____ Fistulae
5. _____ Prolapses       6. _____ None

# Part II: Eradication Strategy

# 8. Strategy for eradication of female circumcision

A clear idea of the inter-relationships between the problem of circumcision and its causes is essential. The situation in Sierra Leone is as indicated in Figure 8.1 (page 70). The causes of the problem stem initially from women strictly and unquestioningly complying with the dictates of their communities. Although this is not directly related to health *per se*, as has been shown in Chapter 6 it seriously affects the quality of a woman's life by creating the health problems listed in categories under C and D in Figure 8.1.

This chapter proposes a strategy for the gradual eradication of circumcision of females wherever this practice still exists, and for the rehabilitation of all circumcised women suffering from its after effects.

A 20-year programme is proposed for appropriate intervention, and although the model proposed is based upon Sierra Leone, it is equally applicable and adaptable to circumstances in other countries.

The proposed strategy has two main areas of impact: *health education*, to increase knowledge of the dangers of circumcision and to correct misguided religious doctrines; and *health care*, to provide early diagnosis, treatment and rehabilitation of the victims of circumcision.

A model budget, which outlines the cost to the nation and shows that the level of expenditure per year per person is well within the means of most countries, is also included.

Before a programme of this magnitude can be launched, it needs an initiating mechanism. The scheme suggested here is one in which a number of capable people, known to have deep commitment to the cause of eradication, are brought together to form an organising committee to carry out preliminary plans prior to formal launching of the programme.

## General goals and objectives of programme

It is important to specify general goals and objectives so as to be able to determine the nature and degree of the intervention required between the causal blocks and the problem of blocks.

69

**Figure 8.1** Interrelationship between the Problem and its Causes

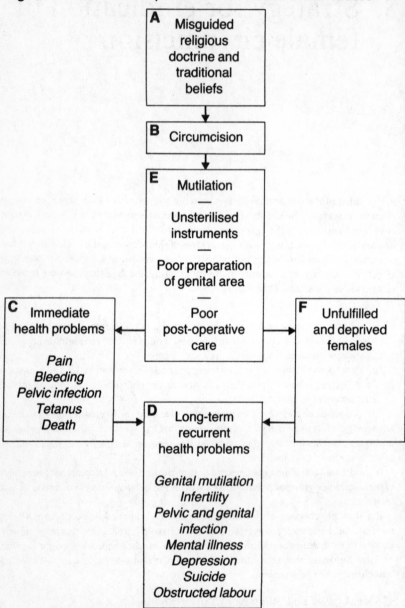

Cause **A** is thus related to the problems in **C** and **D** through links **B** and **E**. Clearly, without **B**, causes **E** and **F** cannot exist and the health problems **C** and **D** will disappear

**Goals:**
1) To eradicate the practice of female circumcision in Sierra Leone.
2) To help cure all those still suffering from the effects of past circumcision, and rehabilitate them for a fuller and happier life in their communities.
Other specific objectives to be defined.

**Objectives (A) Outcome**
1) To reduce the percentage of the female population undergoing circumcision to 8% over a 20-year period by instituting programmes leading to a progressive decline in the practice over four-year periods as shown in Table 8.2.
2) To achieve zero mortality rate amongst women and children undergoing circumcision within one year of the programme commencing.
3) To improve the health and well-being of those already adversely affected by circumcision, so that by the end of the plan period 75% of those affected would be fully rehabilitated by having all infections treated and cured and, as far as possible, other physical disabilities arising from circumcision corrected by medical or surgical intervention.

**Objectives (B) Behavioural**
1) a. Non-Christian women in the community to challenge the provisions of the religious laws which compel them to submit to circumcision, so that within four years of the commencement of the programme in each Province, a strong community resistance to circumcision will have been established.
b. By year 16 of the programme parents in the Province will no longer send their daughters to womanhood-training societies which still practice circumcision.
2) By year 4, religious non-Christian leaders, elders of non-Christian communities and influential non-Christian politicians in each Province to review and reject those provisions of their religious laws that call for female circumcision.
3) *Digbas* or circumcision society priestesses to stop circumcising new recruits entering their societies for training, but to continue to emphasize other, beneficial aspects of womanhood training.
4) All women and children who have been circumcised to seek and receive medical help by the end of the programme period.

Table 8.1
Programme for proposed interventions

| Sector | Target groups |
|---|---|
| Health care | All circumcised women suffering from disabilities as a result of the operation |
| Health education: | |
| sub-section I | Adults at home, on farms, in markets; school children and social leaders |
| sub-section II | *Digbas*, *Sowies* and other *Bundo* officials |

Table 8.2
Sierra Leone: % of women to be persuaded against female circumcision by area and year of programme

| Province | % of total female population in 1985 census | Health Education: Sub-sectors I and II Elimination of circumcision Years of Programme | | | | | Health Care Rehabilitation targets Years of Programme | | | | |
|---|---|---|---|---|---|---|---|---|---|---|---|
| | | 0–4 | 5–8 | 9–12 | 13–16 | 17–20 | 0–4 | 5–8 | 9–12 | 13–16 | 17–20 |
| Northern | 37.1 | 60 | 80 | 90 | 95 | 100 | 70 | 75 | 75 | 75 | 75 |
| Eastern | 26.4 | — | 70 | 80 | 85 | 80 | — | 75 | 75 | 75 | 75 |
| Southern | 21.4 | — | — | 60 | 70 | 80 | — | — | 70 | 75 | 75 |
| Western | 15.1 | — | — | — | 70 | 80 | — | — | — | 70 | 75 |
| Reduction over action period based on total population of women | | 22.3 | 48.2 | 67.4 | 83.2 | 87.5 | n.app. | n.app. | n.app. | n.app. | n.app |

n.app. = not applicable.

72

The Health Care Programme should be run in association with the Local Health Centres, which need improved facilities. The Health Education programme should be undertaken in conjunction with the Local Education Authorities and representatives of Extra-Mural and Extension Services of the University. There should be shifts of emphasis in the programme and relocation of personnel and funds as the need for them changes with the success of the eradication drive.

The Health Care Programme is intended to be a rehabilitation programme and should be run simultaneously with the Health Education Programme. It should include both counselling and medical services. Strong back-up facilities must be maintained throughout the programme. There should be a six month interval between the implementation of the two sub-sectors of the Health Education Programme. Sub-sector I is designed to begin at the same time as the Health Care Programme, that is, immediately the Provincial Council, which is empowered to launch the Programmes, has been set up.

## Programme phases

It will be necessary to phase the programme to provide opportunities for periodic evaluation and revision of strategy where necessary as experience is gained during implementation of each phase.

Five phases are recommended over the 20 year period. The first phase (year 1–4) should involve implementation of both the Health Education and Health Care programmes in one only of the four Provinces. Phase two (year 4–8) to be launched in a second Province. Phase three (year 8–12) in a third and finally (year 12–16) the programme can be extended into the fourth Province. The fifth phase (year 16–20) to involve a comprehensive evaluation of the programme while on-going activities continue in all Provinces. For Sierra Leone, it is proposed that the programme begins in the Northern Province, where links with tradition are presumed to be strongest.

A summary of activities for each phase and the anticipated achievements at the end of each phase are given in Tables 8.3–8.7.

Phase I: (Year 1–4)

a) Formal adoption of National Organizing Committee; training of personnel; start of orientation programmes in capital city.
b) Implementation of Health Education Programme (HEP) sub-sectors I and II (of Table 8.1) in area one (Northern Province).
c) Implementation of the Health Care Programme (HCP) in area one.
d) First 4-year evaluation.

Table 8.3
   Anticipated results targeted achievements % reduction

| New Incidence (NI) cases reduced by | Continuing Cases (CC) for rehabilitation | Health Educational Sector I needs (ESI) | Health Educational Sector II needs (ESII) |
|---|---|---|---|
| 60% | 70% | 100% | 60% |

Phase II: (Year 5–8)

a) Implementation of HEP I and II in area two (Eastern Province).
b) Implementation of HCP in area two.
c) Continuing programmes in area one.
d) Second 4-year evaluation of programmes in both areas.

Table 8.4
Estimated Reduction

| Area (Province) | NI % | CC % | ES-I needs % | ES-II needs % |
|---|---|---|---|---|
| One (Northern) | 80 | 75 | 100 | 80 |
| Two (Southern) | 70 | 75 | 100 | 80 |

Phase III: (Year 9–12)

a) Implementation of HEP I and II in area three (Southern Province).
b) Implementation of HCP in area three.
c) Continuing programmes in areas one and two.
d) Third 4-year evaluation programmes in the three areas.

Table 8.5
Estimated Reduction

| Area (Province) | NI % | CC % | ES-I needs % | ES-II needs % |
|---|---|---|---|---|
| One (Northern) | 90 | 75 | 100 | 90 |
| Two (Southern) | 80 | 75 | 100 | 80 |
| Three (Eastern) | 60 | 70 | 100 | 60 |

Phase IV: (Year 13–16)

a) Implementation of HEP I and II in area four (Western Province).
b) Implementation of HCP in area four.
c) Continuing programmes in areas one, two and three.
d) Policy statement from government on desirability of discontinuing female circumcision.
e) Fourth 4-year evaluation in all four areas.

Table 8.6
Estimated Reduction

| Area (Province) | NI % | CC % | ES-I needs % | ES-II needs % |
|---|---|---|---|---|
| One (Northern) | 95 | 75 | 100 | 95 |
| Two (Eastern) | 85 | 75 | 100 | 85 |
| Three (Southern) | 70 | 75 | 100 | 70 |
| Four (Western) | 70 | 70 | 100 | 70 |

Phase V: (Year 17–20)

a) Continuing programmes in areas one, two, three and four.
b) Institution of laws banning female circumcision.
c) Commencement of comprehensive evaluation programme.

Table 8.7
Estimated Reduction

| Area<br>(Province) | NI<br>% | CC<br>% | ES-I<br>needs % | ES-II<br>needs % |
|---|---|---|---|---|
| One (Northern) | 100 | 75 | 100 | 100 |
| Two (Eastern) | 90 | 75 | 100 | 95 |
| Three (Southern) | 80 | 75 | 100 | 95 |
| Four (Western) | 80 | 75 | 100 | 100 |

It is expected that both the Health Education Sub-sectors (Table 8.1) will become unnecessary after four years of operation in each area/Province. It will have to be assumed that any who remain unconverted after this period may never be converted however long the programme is maintained. Table 8.2, therefore, indicates that there will be no need for this programme at the end of phase one (i.e. 100% reduction). It is also predicted that, under a strong health-care programme, rehabilitation cases will be reduced by 70% in area one (Northern Province) over the same period; and that cases of newly circumcised females will be reduced by 60%.

It is proposed that in Phase IV an active campaign should be started by a group of concerned citizens. Such a group should include experts in law, gynaecology, psychiatry, traditional religions, social science and economics as well as labour matters. They should press relentlessly for some policy statement from government as a first step to discontinuing the practice, using evidence from materials and information obtained from The National Council of the Eradication Programme. During the final phase of the programme, the aim should be for the campaign to have gathered sufficient momentum to be able to press successfully for a law to be passed (in Sierra Leone in the House of Representatives) banning female circumcision throughout the country, such law to include strong legal deterrents enforceable upon any person involved, directly or indirectly, in future performance of such an operation.

The proposed evaluation of the programme during its final phase should include an assessment of the effectiveness of the collaboration between the groups participating in the project. The Ministries of Health, Social Welfare and Education will be encouraged to use the programme period to organize in-service training for their public health, and family planning staff, social workers, and extension service personnel, so that appropriate elements of the health and educational programmes necessary to deal with outstanding problems when the four phases formally end are incorporated into their regular programmes.

## Resources and financial support

The programme will need the support and blessing of appropriate ministries, for example, health development, social welfare and education etc., which should be encouraged to assist in seeking international assistance for the supply of materials, experts, or consultants.

The World Bank, WHO, UNICEF, UNDP, IPPF and World Council of Churches are organizations which may be willing to assist and should be approached. It will be vital to obtain the support of key national figures if the programme is to succeed. Recommended personalities are: the Head of State, and the traditional rulers of the country. The programme should be administered by an independent national body, but the programme base should, for example, be in the Ministry of Social Welfare, with the Ministry of Health having special responsibilities. In Sierra Leone, the Ministry of Social Welfare has existing manpower resources, institutional framework and a budget for the care of Distressed Persons which could be used as a nucleus for the programme.

Funds from participating local and international organizations should be channelled through the national body to an executing body within the appropriate ministry.

# 9. Organization and administration of eradication programme

## The Organizing Committee

An organizing committee, consisting of six to twelve citizens known to be committed to the goal of eradicating female circumcision, capable and willing to serve, should be formed as soon as there is some local focus around which they have a common interest. This may be through membership of study group meetings, at clinical meetings of the local planned parenthood association, or meetings of sub-committees of medical and nurses associations, parent-teachers' associations, or national committees of various kinds, particularly if one exists on traditional practice affecting the health of women and children. In the ideal situation, where groups currently fighting for the eradication of the problem already exist these groups should be mobilized into the organizing committee.

The organizing committee should be ready to assume a catalytic role. Membership could be extended to include such relevant groups as planned parenthood associations, Christian and social welfare organizations. In Sierra Leone, for example, the Medical Women's Association (SLMWA), National Committee on Traditional Practices (SLNCTP) affecting the health of women and children in Africa, the Medical and Dental Association (SLMDA), the Nurse/Midwife Association (SLNMA) and, of course, the Planned Parenthood Association (SLPPA), all have competent members ready to co-operate in effecting such a programme.

A series of preliminary meetings of the organizing committee, to study the overall programme strategy and understand its implications will be necessary, as will preliminary consultations with the government and with overseas organizations known to be sympathetic to the objectives of the programme. The aim of consultations with overseas organizations should be to obtain promises of support funds and expert personnel. This will serve as a morale booster for the programme, and also provide the committee with a better chance of obtaining support from their government and head of state, in so far as an interest in the problem from international circles can be demonstrated and that therefore the country will not be alone in its efforts to eradicate the practice.

The organizing committee should devote a two-week period preceding the initiation of the programme to drawing up a constitution for the setting up of a national body. An appropriate name for such a body, which indicates the full intentions of the programme, is *The National Council for the Welfare of Women*. The Committee should also make recommendations for the appointment to the Council of some of its own members, as well as representatives from the appropriate government ministries (for example, social welfare, health, education etc.) and other influential and concerned local citizens, and SLNCTP members. It should negotiate for space within or near to, for example, the Ministry of Social Welfare; secure agreed transfer of staff and confirm funding with the government, and international and local organizations.

## The National Council

This body should be formally inaugurated when arrangements have been completed for launching the programme, and should replace the organizing committee and take over its responsibilities.

At its first meeting the National Council should:

1. endorse the organizing committee's actions during the planning stage — particularly in so far as obtaining initial government approval is concerned — and confirm promises of international support;

2. ratify its constitution;

3. confirm appointment of members and of the elected chairperson.

The Council should be the programme's chief administrative authority and should set up its administrative machinery as soon as possible in order to avoid the development of negative tendencies and inactivity common to organizations that fail to move quickly. To this end the Council should:

1. recruit its own local and international staff;

2. arrange for secondment of personnel from participating ministries — where feasible;

3. organize initial training of key personnel;

4. establish facilities at Council headquarters for periodic training courses and annual workshops.

The Council's policy-making body should reside in a Board of Management headed by the Chairperson. Additionally, there should be an executive wing comprising a core of professional and administrative staff, which will be accountable to the Board of Management and constitute the chief pressure group co-ordinating and working with community support groups in the propaganda and legal areas. The head of the executive wing should be either a professionally, medically-trained national with public health experience or a social worker with a social science qualification and wide experience in health care and medical welfare.

On assuming authority for the executive of the programme, the Council will determine how it intends to organize its association or co-ordination with other organizations in the health and welfare areas and will draw up procedures for disseminating information to such organizations and to the public at large. The Council should keep in close and constant touch with other organizations and government agencies in particular, with the relevant and appropriate ministries, in order to ensure that any developments which may affect the smooth running of the programme may be known without delay. On p. 80 is a model, based on Sierra Leone's situation, for the organizational structure to be operated by the Council. Appointments to Provincial Councils (or their equivalents in other countries) and their committees will also be the National Council's responsibility, but such bodies should be allowed sufficient autonomy to enable them to act swiftly on matters of urgency without being required to refer to headquarters. The Provincial Councils (or their equivalents) will, however, be required to report on their activities to the National Council on a regular basis.

The National Council will also be responsible for:

1. clearly delineating the terms of reference for Provincial Councils (or their equivalents);

2. clearly defining staff duties;

3. ensuring that all participating staff is fully orientated into the programmes objectives, philosophy and limitations; this exercise to be carried out either at the National headquarters, or the nearest Provincial (etc.) offices;

4. in-service training of Council staff.

## Provincial Councils (or their equivalents)

Each Provincial Council should be run by a local Board (of Elders in Sierra Leone) appointed by the National Council on the recommendation of the Provincial Council. This Board should comprise a Director and a small staff to be appointed by the National Council with the approval of the Provincial Council. The Director to function as the chief co-ordinator of all the activities in his/her province, with a budget which should include provision for the recruitment of specialists in areas not covered by a Research Unit (see p. 90). A Chairman of the Provincial Council will direct the proceedings of the Council's meetings.

As soon as possible, the Provincial Council should prepare a list of suitable, local volunteers, to be recommended to the National Council for appointment as members of the Community Education Action Committee and Provincial Health Care Committee. Each of these committees will have a budgetary vote for running those sections of the programme with which they will be involved. The Provincial Council will be responsible for recommending to the National Council suitable candidates to serve as local representatives, and to encourage and supervise the formation of community support groups (see p. 81 for an example of organizational structure). Each Provincial Council should be represented on the National Council by its Chairman, Board Director and a number of elected members to be agreed upon with the National Council.

Provincial Council committees should consist of workers who have been trained and received orientation for their special roles; they should elect their own leaders and schedule their meetings and field activities to meet the objectives of the strategy. These committees should instruct groups working under them, and these groups must report back to their committee. The committees are the tools of the movement, and should have enough flexibility in the supervision of groups working under them so that they will be fully aware of the pressures of their responsibilities and be driven towards greater efficiency and achievement.

**Figure 9.1** Organizational Structure of the National Council for the Welfare of Women

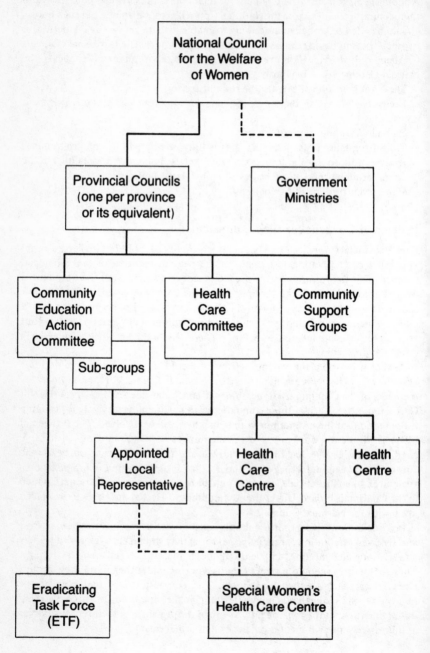

To ensure adequate communication and feedback is maintained between the committees and groups in each Provincial Council (or its equivalent) periodic meetings, briefing sessions and seminars should be arranged on a regular basis.

**Remuneration**
Leaders of committees/groups should receive a salary from the National Council; members of committees/groups should receive honoraria.

## Example of organizational structure:

1. **The National Council for the Welfare of Women**, supported by appropriate ministries. This body to appoint:

2. **The Provincial Councils**, or their equivalents (for Sierra Leone four Provincial Councils one for each of the four Provinces will be appointed). Under each of these Councils will be:

3. i) a **Community Education Action Committee**, which will appoint its own sub-groups;
   ii) a **Health Care Committee**,
   iii) **Community Support Groups**, responsible for a **Health Centre** and a **Health Care Centre**.

4. The **Community Education Action Committee**, in conjunction with the **Health Care Centre** will be responsible for appointing the Eradicating Task Force (ETF).

5. The **Health Centre** and the **Health Care Centre** will be jointly responsible for setting up and running the **Special Women's Health Care Centre**.

6. All Provincial Council Committees and the Special Women's Health Care Centre to work in conjunction with the appointed **Local Representative**.

# 10. Health education and health care: organization and objectives

## Health education

The programme in this sector should include special training of all personnel in the Provincial Council committees, who, from time to time, will require their knowledge and skills updated. After initial training, however, the committees must address themselves to their respective functions.

A *Community Education Action Committee* (CEAC) is to be established by the Provincial Council, to carry out the Health Education Programme, Sub-sectors I and II. The CEAC must work with and through sub-groups referred to as Eradicating Task Force (ETF) (Figure 9.1). These sub-groups must be carefully chosen and trained and should be the pressure groups enforcing action on all indicated fronts, and monitoring the performance of non-committee recruits.

### Health Education Programme Sub-sector I

The programme has been developed for the following three categories:
1. Adults at home, in the farms, in the market and hospitals and health care centres.
2. Children at schools.
3. Community leaders.
The objectives are as follows:

1) By the end of Year one, in area one (Northern Province), and within the first year of the establishment of Provincial Councils (or their equivalents) in the rest of the country the following should have been achieved:

a) 25% of mothers in seclusion at home, other female members of their households and women working in the fields, who have medical complaints arising from past circumcision, should seek help at the Health Centres. The number should increase to 50% of all such women in Year two, 75% in Year three, and 100% in Year four.

b) By joining community support groups and assisting in enlightening other market women and shoppers and getting signatures and thumbprints for petitions to religious leaders and government 25% of market women should have a full understanding of injuries and diseases resulting from circumcision. This number should increase to 50% in Year two, 70% in Year three, and 100% in Year four of the programme in each Province.

2) By the end of Year three following the introduction of the Health Education Sector 1 in each Province, 70%, and by the end of Year four, 100%, of the local secondary school children should be expected to show an understanding of the health risks of circumcision by initiating debates in and between schools and mounting field projects to inform neighbouring communities about the problem.

3) By the end of Year four in area one (Northern Province) and year 16 everywhere else, religious and political leaders and organizations should understand the pressing problems of women in the communities by supporting moves to bring about legislation to ban circumcision.

The CEAC will need six sub-groups (ETFs) who may also be CEAC members. The sub-groups may be named alphabetically from A to F: A–D will be assigned to citizens in category one, sub-group E to citizens in category two, and sub-group F to citizens in category three.

Because it is important for leaders to know what is being planned in their communities before it happens, sub-groups A to D should visit their assigned citizens at the same time as sub-group F contacts citizens in category three. The idea is not to seek permission but to inform. These two approaches should precede the approach to category two targets by two weeks, in order to give the community time to adjust to the shock of invasion into their social castles and make them less unwilling to consider the idea of instructing their children in ways which will lead to their rejection of elements of their culture. It has been shown that parents will be more supportive of the inclusion of controversial contents in their education when a need for their inclusion has been clearly established and communicated (Kunstel, 1978).

The strategy proposed is as follows:

*Sub-group A:* will focus attention on house-to-house discussions with mothers, and other female members of the household, using pictures and posters. They will also encourage those who have medical complaints arising from past circumcision to seek help at the Health Centre.

*Sub-group B:* will focus attention on the women working on the farms and in fields, using posters and pictures.

*Sub-group C:* will work among market women and shoppers at various market sites in each Province using mobile vans equipped with cinematograph projectors and slides. Moving and still pictures will be used during talks to market audience, to bring home dramatically and realistically the injuries and diseases resulting from circumcision.

*Sub-group D:* will concentrate on patients already attending the Health Care Centres. Slides and films will be used in short instruction sessions in the out-patient waiting room.

*Sub-group E:* will visit all schools in the Province to which it is assigned, giving supplementary lectures, with slides, and providing wall-posters for permanent display. This will encourage the introduction of courses on health hazards among the female population. By the third year following the introduction of HEP 1 in each Province, 70% of the local secondary schools will have received information on the health risks of circumcision. By the sixth year all schools will have this information included in their curricula.

*Sub-group F:* will visit Imams in the mosques, politicians in their constituency offices, leaders of Islamic Welfare Organizations, other non-Christian and some Christian organizations, and explain to them the serious health problems of women in their communities and describe the dangers to which women are exposed. The group will ask for their support in bringing about change in those aspects of their religious teachings which compel women to undergo circumcision.

It should be sub-group F's responsibility to mobilize other pressure groups consisting of concerned citizens, members of SLNCTP, experts on the legal rights of women, obstetrical and gynaecological specialists, economic labour force experts, specialists in traditional religions and social science experts, in order to influence public opinion and stimulate representations to the head of state, cabinet ministers and so on, to seek first a policy statement and later the institution of a law to ban female circumcision in the country.

The CEAC sub-groups should use materials supplied by the Research Unit (see p. 90). Adults in category one should be taught individually, or in small home groups; visits should be repeated until comprehension and positive reactions are achieved. In the markets and hospitals, locations should be selected so that groups attracted will be as homogenous as possible in terms of age, interest and discussion level. Each market place should be visited monthly, and posters should be replaced by new ones at each visit.

Discussions with citizens in category three should proceed with great caution, sub-group visits should be less frequent, and remain at the individual contact level during the first year.

The programme for citizens in category two should focus on upper primary and secondary school classes. It should be built around the existing science curriculum and based on the assumption that children in these classes (4–7 primary, 1–6 secondary, who will be between the ages 8–18) will be receptive to learning more about their bodies. Instruction and information should be orientated towards showing how indirect and weak is the link of circumcision to Islam; how the practice existed before Islam came to Africa; and why it should now be dissociated from the religion. They should also explain concepts in animism and show how the sanctity of human life must take precedence over the sanctity of other beings and things.

Outside experts' visits should be reinforced by visits of the CEAC sub-group E assigned to schools, and by the support of science teachers in each school involved. These teachers should receive initial training at the Provincial Council office, along lines prescribed by the Research Unit (see p. 90), and attend special annual workshops at the National Council's Headquarters. After initial training, the teachers should be in a position to use materials supplied by the Research Unit, including audio-visual materials, and also provide back-up inputs carefully programmed for introduction during normal lessons, periods for news and views, debating sessions, question/answer periods and for replying to students questions outside of lesson periods. Posters should be permanently displayed on classroom walls. Relevant booklets and teachers' guides developed by the Research Unit should be readily available at the Provincial Council office under the control of the Community Education Action Committee.

It is important for teachers to give students and pupils exercises which present real-life problems, for example, dealing with the decision of parents to send them for circumcision; facing submission to and return from circumcision; reaction to emotional stress; importance of medical attention when physically injured after the operation. Such problems should be discussed in the light of the ethical, social and medical issues involved. Skills to sharpen the students' decision-making ability and increase their interest in self-care and self-protection should form part of the education process. The school must act as liaison with the Health Education Action Committee and the Health Care Committee to provide protection for their pupils/students when cases requiring civil or criminal action in courts occur.

### Health Education Programme Sub-sector II

In Sierra Leone this programme is to be directed to the *Digbas/Sowies* (Priestesses) and other circumcision society officials and initiates, and appropriate persons/groups in other countries. Planning of this sub-sector programme should commence at the end of the first year of activities. This should include training of staff recruited for this programme. Twenty-five recruits will be required, who have had the benefit of the HEP 1 programme, all to be drawn from the circumcision societies. New recruits will be admitted every four months, and will receive three-months in-depth training, the details and course structure to be designed by the Research Unit. Training will be given by the Community Education Action Committee (CEAC), and should be in the local languages of the region. Recruits should be chosen who are well respected in the society, but young enough to feel excited by the challenges of the problem. They should be screened for certain desirable attributes such as maturity, personal charm, persuasiveness, and persistence.

If the plan is carefully operated, 20% of the circumcision societies would have ETFs operating within their precincts by the end of the second year of the programme. By the end of the third year, the squads should be in 40% of the societies; and by Year four in 60%.

The training programme for the ETF should include:

1. human hygiene;
2. importance of asepsis in surgery;
3. diseases contracted as a result of circumcision.
4. obstetric complications, resulting from injury due to circumcision;
5. diagnosis of potentially fatal cases after circumcision and procedures for referrals to Health Centres and hospitals;
6. recognition of circumcision complications in old cases and procedures for referrals to the local Health Centre;
7. simple treatment and management of vaginal injury;
8. simple emergency procedures in medicine;
9. rudiments of human behaviour;

10. methods of negotiating, particularly with intransigent groups;
11. art of compromise;
12. art of perseverance;
13. persuasive approaches to social problem-solving;
14. nutritional values of different local foodstuffs.

The objectives are as follows:

**HEP Sub-sector II**
(1) By the end of Year two, 20% of all societies in the North (area one) should, through instruction and guidance from an ETF, learn about and practice:
(i) improved sanitation;
(ii) improved surgical procedures.
There should also have been achieved:
(iii) partial success in persuading the Digbas and the senior members of the society to discuss the rationale of circumcision and its associated problems.
(2) By the end of Year four, the following situations should exist in 60% of all the societies in the North (area one):
(iv) full hygienic conditions;
(v) full knowledge of the dangers of circumcision through presentation of cases and evidence, which should include posters, pictures and slides;
(vi) agreement on modification of the role of the society in the community.
(3) By the end of Year six the following should have been achieved:
(vii) the practice of circumcision should stop in 20% of the societies in the North (area one), and this should increase to 80% by the end of Year eight.
(4) The same level of achievement should occur in the East (area two) by Year eight, in the South (area three) by Year twelve, and in the West (area four) by Year sixteen.
(5) By the end of the planned period, the practice of female circumcision should be eliminated.

As recruits complete their training they are to be organized into ETFs groups of five. Each Task Force (ETF) will be given an identity number and sent to a circumcision society in the Province to start a process of change within the society's precincts. They should maintain the dignity of the society to which they are assigned, and draw attention not only to the negative, but also to the beneficial aspects of the society's activities.

Aspects of womanhood training in the circumcision societies should be strengthened and additional training in child-care and proper nutrition should be given; in particular nutrition for mothers during their first pregnancy will be taught. This should reduce the number of mothers who give birth to weak babies.

There are a number of circumcision sessions each year in most societies. The ETFs should, after each session, be able to feed back information of their experience to the Provincial Community Education Action Committee, through the local representative of the town in which they live. They should also keep records of recruits entering the circumcision society each session and make note of the level of their acceptability within the societies. Such information will form the basis of revised strategies which, if necessary, will be developed by the Education Committee and the ETFs themselves at joint meetings which should be convened as often as possible and preferably prior to Task Forces taking up new assignments or returning to a new circumcision session, in their former stations.

## Health care programme

Within six months of the start of the programme, the National Council, in collaboration with the Ministry of Health, should institute measures to update existing Health Centres, providing a special women's care department within these Centres. The medical officer in charge of this department should work closely with the Provincial Council and the local Health Care Committee.

By Year three of the programme in any area the Council should have its own special Women's Care Clinic in four main towns in each area/Province, and by Year six, the Council should have a special Women's Care Clinic within a radius of 25 miles of any circumcision society.

### Objectives

This programme should be directed towards already circumcised women who have any disabilities, illness or other conditions directly related to their circumcision.

The Health Care Committee (HCC) appointed by the National Council on the recommendation of the Provincial Council, should be responsible for executing this programme, but will be accountable to the Provincial Council and ultimately to the National Council.

Examination, treatment and referral procedures prepared by the Research Unit should be adopted (see page 90). Initially, all examination and treatment should be carried out at Health Centres, which should be upgraded during the first six months of the programme in the specific area or Province, to provide a special department with the necessary facilities for running the programme. By the sixth year, however, independent Women's Health Care Centres should be established and fully staffed in order to take over the responsibilities for these special cases from the Health Centres.

The women referred for diagnosis of their health problems by the ETFs or Community Education Action Committee or those who visit the Health Centres on their own initiative (see Figure 10.1) should be categorized according to their health conditions as follows:

*Category I:* Women recently circumcised suffering pain, urinary infections, and showing signs and symptoms of anaemia.
*Category 2:* Women complaining of primary infertility, dyspareunia due to small introitus, urinary infections and other local pains.
*Category 3:* Women complaining of secondary infertility, torn perineum after first delivery, signs and symptoms of vaginal prolapse, habitual uterine wastage due to urinary infections caused by unsuspected urinary fistulae, and women with recognized vaginal and rectal fistulae.
*Category 4:* Women suffering from mental depression.

**Figure 10.1** Diagnosis and Treatment of Health Problems Resulting from Circumcision

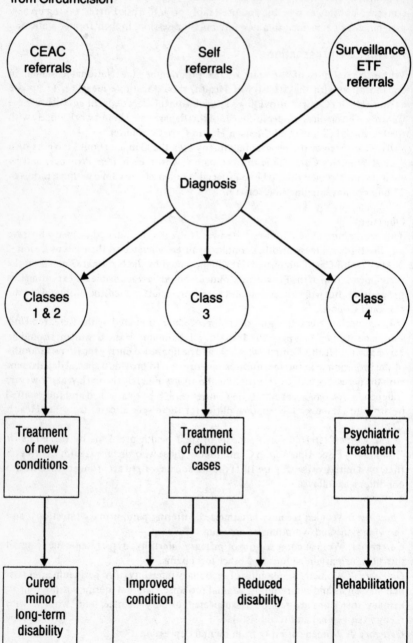

All examinations, treatment and counselling, and any other relevant data to be recorded under the four categories defined and sent to the Research Unit for analysis.

The severity of each case will be assessed and recorded on a scale of 0–5, 5 indicating greatest severity. Categories 1 and 2 to be treated as soon as they are diagnosed by appropriate medication or surgery or both, and the patient on recovery, recorded as cured. In the event of the discovery of more serious conditions of patients in Categories 1 and 2 they will be tranferred to Category 3. Patients in Categories 3 and 4 will be screened periodically, preferably monthly, to detect progress; patients in Category 4 will be referred to a psychiatry consultant.

**Administrative Objectives**

1) The National Council should establish good working relations with the Ministry of Social Welfare (or its equivalent) and obtain its input for preparing operational plans within two weeks of the programme's launching.

2) Complete arrangements for the secondment of specialists' staff from all the relevant ministries (for example, in addition to social welfare, health, and education) by the third week.

3) Recruitment of national expert staff and auxiliary staff should begin in the fourth week; all will be at their posts by the end of the second month.

4) Recruitment of specialist international staff should be completed by the sixth month.

5) Orientation and initial training of key personnel for the Health Education Programmes (sub-sectors I and II) and the Health Care Programme (HCP) for Programme Phase one should be completed by the end of the third month.

6) By the end of the sixth month, the National Council should be in a position to complete the setting up of its organizational structure.

For phase one, the following should have been set up:*

a) *Northern Provincial Council (NPC):* to be responsible to the National Council for all matters concerned with the input of all programmes in that Province.

b) *Northern Community Education Action Committee:* to be directly responsible to the NPC and be charged with the task of executing Health Education sub-sectors I and II. The Task Forces to be specially trained by, and to assist the Committee will be employed in the execution of the Health Education programme, Sector 2.

c) *Northern Health Care Committee:* to be directly responsible to the NPC and charged with the task of carrying out the Health Care programme for the Province.

d) *A small local office in each town of the Province:* to be manned by a local representative working under the direction of the Community Education Action Committee (CEAC). The duties of the representative include acting as liaison between individuals and groups working for the Council, as well as providing information about the Council's activities to people requiring them.

*Although the following model refers specifically to Sierra Leone it can easily be adapted for other countries.

7) By the end of 12 months, community support groups would begin to appear and take part in publishing and other campaigns.

8) Provincial bodies similar to those in the Northern Province should be set up as follows: by the end of the fifth year in the Eastern Province; by the end of the ninth year in the Southern Province; by the end of the twelfth year in the Western Province.

**Operational Methods**

*Approach:* As explained under "Programme Phases" the plan should be put into operation first in the Northern Province/first area, then extended to the other three Provinces/areas. An evaluation of the programme should be carried out, based on records collected during the phase period at the end of four years. The result of this evaluation will guide the implementation of the other phases of the project.

Six months before activities start in an area/Province, the attitudes and customs in the area/Province, with regard to organized groups sponsored from outside should be investigated. During this period the National Council should obtain information on working patterns in agricultural and mining communities in the province, traditional laws, and any provincial behavioural characteristics which could be exploited to the advantage of the programme. Simultaneously, a survey of elders (or their equivalent) in the area/Province should be conducted to identify persons of appropriate calibre whom the National Council might invite to form the Provincial Council. Accommodation for the office of the Provincial Council should also be investigated.

By the end of this period, the National Council should appoint the first (Northern) Province Council; the programme director and his/her staff should be appointed and immediately receive orientation at the National Council's Headquarters. The programme to begin as soon as orientation is complete.

# Research unit

The two components of the proposed programme namely: the Health Educational Programme (HEP), and the Health Care Programme (HCP), are to be supported by a multi-disciplinary research unit. This unit will provide educational materials and curricula for the two Educational Programme sectors, and medical procedures and training methods for the Health Care Programme.

The research unit to be led by a Consultant of reputable international standing in the health education field, assisted by a deputy, who should be a specialist in gynaecology. Additionally, three recognized researchers, one each specializing in psychology, health education and social science, should be appointed to assist the Consultant and his/her deputy, plus six research assistants in the fields of education and health. The team should be appointed on four-year renewable contracts.

*Tasks of Research Unit*

1) Conduct surveys on circumcision of females.

2) Supervise evaluation records.

3) Develop educational materials including booklets for children, carefully graded for different age groups.

4) Prepare leaders' guide for teachers.

5) Prepare curricula with strong anti-circumcision elements for schools and adult classes.

6) Develop questionnaires and evaluate testing methods and interview schemes; also draw up in anti-circumcision campaign petition formats.

7) Prepare medical examination procedures.

8) Test and evaluate specific radio and visual aids intended for use in the programme.

9) Commission and review plays supporting eradication which are to be written and produced in the local languages.

10) To receive all completed questionnaires and signed petitions, compile records from these and periodically evaluate and analyse.

At the end of the first four years the Research Unit to have studied all the records in its possession and prepared a first report on the overall changes achieved in the attitude of the community towards female circumcision; changes in the number of those enrolled at circumcision societies; and recovery levels at the health centres. These figures will be compared with the objectives set for the first four-year period. Subsequent evaluation reports should be prepared at four year intervals, based on records collected over the previous four years. A comprehensive evaluation of the programme to commence in the seventeenth year covering the entire plan-period. All evaluation reports should be discussed at the Provincial level before being submitted to the National Council for review.

The Research Unit should normally have access to the Provincial Councils and their Committees, to which it is expected to act as education and health consultant.

**Supplementary activities**
The various provincial community support groups formed with the encouragement of the Provincial Councils should be charged with the organization of community activities to raise funds for the National Council, provide a base for appeals to government and the community, and draw up plans which should include a time-table for achieving a law banning female circumcision. These groups may be organized in branches specializing in fund raising, mobilizing public opinion, and legal matters, etc.

*Fund-raising:* this activity is necessary to ensure continued financial support for the programme at a level required to maintain its effectiveness. Even where government and/or international funds are available, it is important to tap local resources to enable the National Council to deal with emergency situations, carry out bridging programmes or prepare for the day when possible conflicts of objectives between donors and the Council may force it to proceed with the programme independently.

Fund-raising activities could take the form of: luncheon sales, discos, moonlight picnics, sponsored walks, dinner and dances, raffles, flag days, variety shows, plays etc. Funds realized from these activities should be sent to the National Council's treasury at its headquarters.

*Mobilizing public opinion:* entails liaison with members of sub-group F (see p. 84) working on Education Sub-sector I, who have gained experience and understanding in discussions with traditional and religious leaders. Material for use by these groups is to be supplied by the Research Unit, including questionnaires and petition forms. The press, radio and television should be utilized and as well as any opportunity at local social functions where audience interest could be exploited. Such branches should assist the Research Unit by circulating evaluation forms and ensuring these are answered and returned. They should give particular attention to the completion of petition forms which will be regularly monitored to determine the opportune time to launch a national appeal for a law to ban circumcision of women.

*Legal Matters:* involve keeping a close watch on situations which need legal attention. It should be made known to the women in the community that there are friends among them who are willing to protect their rights if and when they wish to exercise such rights. Co-operation with the Health Education Action Committee and the Health Education Committee is necessary in order that problem cases can be directed to the legal branch of the community support group. When it is known that legal advice is available, a slow but steady increase in the numbers of women and children who will feel brave enough to refuse circumcision and who need legal and friendly advice and comfort can be expected. With the advance of the programme it may be necessary for a few test cases to be put through the courts; charges of criminal assault can be brought against individuals coming to circumcise women and children against their wishes. The combined circumstances of an aggrieved initiate, an enlightened community and an impartial judiciary may be a dream today, but a reality in the future.

Community support groups should assist in circulating questionnaires and petition forms prepared by the Research Unit and approved by the National Council's Board of Management. Questionnaires should be distributed at the start of each sector of the programme (see Table 8.1) and every six months thereafter; completed sets to be returned to the Research Unit for processing and filing. Participants in Category 1 (adults at home, etc.) of Sub-sector I, will be required to sign/thumb-mark petitions supporting women's fight against circumcision. Participants in Category 3 will also be requested to sign/thumb-mark petitions to be circulated monthly by the CEAC. The Research Unit to compile records of monthly endorsements and test for changes in the level of conviction and in attitudes brought about by the programme. The ETFs records are also to be sent to the Research Unit for analysis at the end of each session.

The School Health Education programme should be tested for achievement at various levels. A questionnaire should be used to collect information from the teachers; students' knowledge and response to health problems should be judged from tests requiring them to answer questions based on potential health problems connected with circumcision. These tests will be drawn up by the Research Unit but conducted by the teachers; test results to be submitted to the Unit.

The Health Care Committee (HCC) working in conjunction with the Health Centre should keep daily records of new cases seen, old cases treated, case histories, time and place of circumcision, treatment given, recovery levels, further referrals if made, and information of the source from which each patient learned of the

Committee's services. All details recorded should be sent each month to the Research Unit.

*Evaluation:* should cover all sectors of activities, down to the supplementary activities. The Health Education Sectors should be evaluated by way of questionnaires developed by the Research Unit. Tests should include achievements of citizens in Categories 1, 2, and 3 in respect of their: a) acquisition of knowledge of selected information; b) development of attitudes and behaviour, such as motivation and willingness to join and participation in community support groups; c) initiation rates; and d) attendance levels at the special Women's Health Care Centres.

# Beneficial results of eradication

## Social

African women are the matrix of their societies. The pillar of strength in many homes, financial wizards in businesses, architects of the family destiny, and the great defenders of traditional practices, some of which are detrimental to their own health and that of their children.

Women play many roles in circumcision societies, some of whose members are Traditional Birth Attendants (TBA), nurse/midwives, herbalists, home economists, artists, craftswomen, traders, business women, teachers etc. Thus, each can teach the young initiates her own special art.

It is well-known that girls who are shortly to be circumcised become anxious, depressed and frightened. Some suffer from diarrhoea, dietary problems or develop unexplained skin eruptions. If circumcision were eradicated probably young girls would gladly go to these societies to be trained in various activities offered. There would be excitement and joy at the prospect of meeting and making life-long friendships with other girls of their own age. Girls from all communities could also join the societies and benefit from the training.

*Types of Training*
1. The nutritional values of locally grown foodstuffs;
2. the importance of a balanced diet and fresh fruits, to prevent malnutrition;
3. the benefits of backyard gardens, to reduce some of the financial burden on the household;
4. the importance of hygiene, sanitation, clean drinking water to prevent the many cases of diarrhoea in developing countries;
5. the identification and methods of dispelling food taboos; for example, the belief that women and children should not eat chicken, but men can. This taboo is typical of patriarchal societies in which custom dictates that the man should have the largest helping and the best food, because he is the breadwinner.
6. the uses of medicinal herbs;
7. the importance of attending ante- and post-natal clinics;
8. the advantages of family planning to space children; some of these girls on leaving the societies go straight to their matrimonial homes;
9. the benefits of breast as compared to bottle-feeding;

10. local foodstuffs that can be used to wean babies;
11. the importance of vaccinations for mothers and babies.

All of these will reduce the load on the Ministry of Health who are severely short-staffed.

Additionally, the home economist/nutritionist experts can teach different ways of cooking, as well as sewing, handcraft, pottery, hair-plaiting and styling, tie and *gara* cloth, crops preservation etc. These crafts can be pursued with considerable financial rewards on leaving the society, giving the woman a degree of financial independence and control.

The sense of social cohesion so produced will reduce the feeling of animosity amongst ethnic groups in which circumcised and uncircumcised women live in close proximity. A reduction in child mortality and morbidity should also become evident, and the complaint of circumcised women that their menfolk prefer uncircumcised women should likewise diminish.

**Health**
1. There will be no post-circumcision complications, but women will be in full control of their bodies and, with unmutilated organs, capable of sexual enjoyment.
2. Labour will be normal and children born without trauma. No development of fistulae and hence no frequent miscarriages. Low maternity and child mortality rates.
3. No vulvar cysts/abscesses, mental depression, frequent divorces and suicides in later life. Under-fertility is greatly reduced women will live a full and healthy life and be able to contribute to the economic progress of the community. Hospital costs for those who need to be admitted for post-circumcision treatment will be greatly reduced. The government can then channel funds previously so used into other urgent areas.

**Economic**
In the last two decades African women have been changing roles. From being predominantly farm support workers, traders, producers of crafts and children, many African women now fill professional positions. In Sierra Leone, the fact that female circumcision is reducing the number of young, fertile women who could contribute to the developing society or fill positions as social reformers, policy makers, industrial workers or administrators, has come as a rude shock. Some Christian groups are outraged by this continuing disregard for the health of women and the waste of human resources involved.

International organizations concerned about the situation have given support to those local health practitioners, welfare workers, practicing midwives, and family-planning workers who have been vocal about the problem and tried to bring the seriousness of the matter to the attention of the public. These groups realize that a country with so large a proportion of unhealthy women can never make the progress towards economic and social development expected of it. Just as Sierra

Leonian women have been the backbone of the traditional economy, so today are they the backbone of areas of the modern, urban economy, controlling the collection and distribution of agricultural goods for up-country sources as well as the retail trading of imported goods.

In the underdeveloped communities of the past, the effects of circumcision and its concomitant health hazards on the traditional economy, even if significant, were impossible to assess.

Absenteeism, or indisposition or loss of an able worker certainly affected output, but the level of productivity usually fluctuated widely as a result of such readily identifiable factors as unfavourable weather, vandalism, pests and crop diseases, and no one was interested in other less obvious, or controversial factors. Today no nation can afford to disregard any problem, no matter how small, which has a potentially disruptive effect on the economy.

An assessment of the economic loss to the community of treating girls who undergo circumcision can be based on the results shown in Table 5.1 of the pilot study. Although 83% of the girls may require medical treatment, not all will have access to it. It is known that about 40–45% of Sierra Leone's nationals receive medical attention from recognized medical centres and units at which they or the government pay for the treatment. It can be estimated, therefore, that the country's economy will have to bear the cost of treating around 37% of all girls undergoing circumcision, and this represents a quite significant proportion of the health budget. The cost of treating older women will be even higher, and when this is added to the loss of output by those in the productive sector the economic repercussions of the problem are obvious.

Modern Sierra Leone — indeed, all developing countries — needs to mobilize all hands possible in order to move out of underdevelopment into a prosperous future. All the women, not just a small proportion of them, must contribute to the fullest extent, and with a healthy and sound mind and body.

The only significant actions known to have been taken to date have come from a small group of doctors working within a social welfare organization. Their work has been directed towards improving the procedures so as to reduce the risk of infection. Nothing has been done to eradicate female circumcision itself or to rehabilitate its victims. Groups within the traditional ruling classes exert strong pressure on policy-makers to ensure they do nothing to upset the traditional system.

The work of these doctors has been only partly successful, even in reducing the incidence of infection. They have been able to work in only one district in the Southern Province where they have ethnic connections. Even so, doctors cannot enter the sacred precincts of the circumcision society unless they are members and, of course, are circumcised. They, therefore, resorted to training society members in surgical procedures and serving as consultants to some societies and are thus available only to deal with emergencies when they arise.

This approach to the problem has clearly been unsatisfactory. The training of the societies' operators and officials should have been taken beyond instructions in hygiene and surgical methods and included teaching them the anatomy of the organs being operated upon. The risks, and the futility of the operation, using living examples of those suffering from mutilation and various disabilities caused by the operation should also have been brought to the attention of those who perform the operation. The many women already circumcised have been neglected in this programme; this is a serious failing.

# 11. Conclusions and recommendations

The practice of circumcising girls and women is entrenched in the socio-cultural life of an undesirably large percentage of women and children in Africa. Except for the activities of the Inter-African Committee on traditional practices affecting the health of women and children, its national committees, and a token display of concern by some other bodies the practice continues unchecked, as a symbol of feminine maturity and subservience. Women have been successfully persuaded to attach special importance to female circumcision, motherhood, and housekeeping, in order to maintain male domination in patriarchal societies.

Circumcision, and many other social and cultural practices are known to be detrimental to women's health and well-being, and to be responsible for keeping the majority of them outside the mainstream of national life. It has been shown that circumcision is part of a complex socio-cultural manipulation. Other facets of this process are evident today in the field of politics, where women are denied equal opportunities with men, in technical training, in business and many other activities.

Yet, it has been observed that the traditional rural woman fears, and has shown resistance to, change. Before marriage and motherhood are possible, she knows she must comply with the dictates of society. She realizes, however, that apart from, and within marriage, motherhood and domesticity, she needs her husband's love and protection. But she is also aware that she must wait patiently until she receives this love and protection, not as the response to her rightful expectations, but as charity. A husband, home and children are status symbols of high value in her society, and she will ensure that she does nothing to endanger her position as potential wife and mother.

In Sierra Leone a childless woman is called a "Cock" (male fowl); as in many other Third World countries only the woman carries the blame for childlessness. The African male is supposed to be a divine gift to the African female, and even if he is azoospermic, a condition of sterility, he still blames the infertility on his wife. Belief in supernatural powers, witchcraft and the occult has tended to deter intelligent assessment of women's conditions; also, religious doctrines are too often applied to frighten women into submission.

Some element of financial gain has influenced circumcision practice in some communities. For the African man in his traditional community, the consciousness that money and other assets give him status and power may lead him to support actions which will increase these assets.

Womens' ignorance about themselves and their rights has been exploited to the extent that many lack the will to be free to be themselves, or the mental outlook to be financially independent. They are conditioned to feel happy and contented only when playing the roles of mother and wife. Cast in this mould, and erected as monuments in societies where their fertility commands great value in the face of high infant mortality, they feel obliged to subject themselves to any practice which they are made to believe will increase their fertility and enhance their assigned roles.

The acceptable image of a woman with a place in society becomes that of one who is circumcised, docile, fertile, marriageable, hardworking, asexual and obedient. The reality of the woman in society, however, is one crippled physically and mentally for the rest of her life. There is urgent need for a socio-cultural revolution to avert the impending danger from mutilation of future generations of African women.

The first step in this revolution must be taken by the women themselves, using their own organizations. They must start by freeing themselves from ignorance, fear and mental servitude. Those women who already know the health hazards of female circumcision should join in the education of their sisters. Only with the involvement of women themselves can programmes and plans for eradication succeed. There have been other socio-cultural revolutions in the world in this century. For example, the practice of burning widows in India (suttee) has been proscribed; binding the feet of Chinese women has been stopped, as has the custom, once practiced by Arab women, of burying their baby girls alive. If others have examined their cultures and cleansed them of practices injurious to the health of their fellow citizens, there is hope that the practice of female circumcision in Africa will be eradicated.

# Recommendations

The overriding recommendation is, of course, the abolition of female circumcision. Because secrecy surrounds the operation and has been maintained amongst those who practice it in order to protect the custom, it is necessary to *expose the practice, educate the community and treat and counsel the victims.*

The programme strategy proposed in Chapters 8, 9 and 10 should be studied to determine how it could best be applied to and implemented by all countries where female circumcision is still carried out. All, or part, of the programme could be adapted for countries other than Sierra Leone. Health planners and concerned groups of health workers and advisers will find the programme useful in reviewing their own national health strategies.

For those who prefer to draw up their own programmes, the Guidelines in this chapter (pp. 99–103) will be of assistance to them. One area where difficulties may be encountered will be raising funds to execute any eradication programme. It may be important to concentrate first on sensitizing both local and international communities; an army of people are needed in the fight against female circumcision. There is no doubt that the heavy weight of international opinion put behind any local effort will provide the moving force necessary to initiate the programme strategy in any particular country.

A general approach to this campaign should involve the following:

1. Raising the issue and passing resolutions against female circumcision at all international and local conferences discussing such topics as health in general, maternal and child health, education and welfare.

2. Seeking support for and organizing international seminars and conferences on female circumcision.

3. Seeking support for the inclusion of female circumcision in WHO's list of ailments and diseases needing an eradication drive.

4. Persuading WHO to have a policy on treatment and rehabilitation of post-circumcision cases.

5. Encouraging womens' organizations worldwide to send petitions to governments of countries that practice female circumcision.

6. Encouraging donors and administrators of multinational and bilateral aid for health care to make the award of such aid conditional upon the inclusion of a plan to eradicate female circumcision.

## Guidelines

**Stage I:** Problem identification:
Explain the problem indicating special circumstances, and special community situations in your country.

**Stage 2**

1. *Problem analysis*
   a) Analyse the problem and say how you will deal with the interrelations between elements of the problem;
   b) Show how you will treat outside influences which directly/indirectly affect the problem.

2. *Goals and objectives*
   a) State general goals;
   b) State specific goals indicating time frames;
   c) State administrative objectives;
   d) State outcome objectives, and include projections.

3. *Support structures for the programme*
   a) Indicate sources of local support;
   b) Indicate possible sources of international support;
   c) Indicate linkages for the structure, e.g. local institutions (private and governmental) international organizations etc.

4. *Programme Phases*
   a) Develop a concept for the operation of the programme, whether a single phase or several phases will be required;
   b) Indicate time frame for each phase, and the sector of the programme to be dealt with under each phase.

## 5. *Programme Organization and Administration*

   a) Draw up an administrative structure similar to that in Figure 9.1;

   b) Make sure that units are created to effect each aspect of the work envisaged to achieve each of the objectives determined in Stage 3. For example, if you want to educate the community you must have a committee education unit. If you want to have an informed community you must have a propaganda unit. There should be some discretion in the setting-up of these units. Too many will be uncontrollable, too few ineffective. It is important, in any case, to have a strong central body at the top of the pyramidal structure, and several people on committees and many workers at the base of the pyramid.

   c) Involve some community leaders in the plan. They must be given a role as they are important in areas of the programmes involving consultations and discussions, persuasions and intimidation of other leaders supporting the practice.

## 6. *Operational Mechanism*

This is where you prepare for the execution of your programme. You should propose the most effective method you feel should be applied to carry out the functions assigned to each unit of the organization.

This should include:

   a) who to train;

   b) training methods;

   c) assignments and posting of personnel;

   d) interview techniques;

   e) research methodology.

## 7. *Evaluation methods* to discover how well the programme is succeeding.

The year 2000 has been set aside by the World Health Organization (WHO) as the year in which the world should attain a reasonable level of health for all its peoples; the slogan "Health for all by the year 2000" has been coined. It will be a great achievement if by that year Africa has banished the scourge of female circumcision and given its women healthy and enjoyable lives.

# Appendix 3

## NOTES TO BUDGET FOR SIERRA LEONE
### Contract Staff

The staff for the **Research Unit** and their payments to be as follows:

| Position | Control Period | Fixed Annual Payment (in United States dollars) |
|---|---|---|
| Research Consultant | | 120,000 |
| Deputy Research Consultant | 4 (part time) | 60,000 |
| Health Education Specialist | 4 (part time) | 48,000 |
| Psychologist | 4 (part time) | 48,000 |
| Social Science Expert | 4 (part time) | 48,000 |
| Supplementary Staff (6) | 4 (full time) | 112,000 |
| Secretarial Staff | – (full time) | 72,000 |
| Office Expenses | – (full time) | 40,000 |
| | | *548,000* |

### Other Consultants

Other consultants to be hired as required for specialities not covered in the Research Unit and Health Centres, as follows:

| | (Leones*/hour) |
|---|---|
| Psychiatrist | 400 |
| Evaluation Specialists | 500 |
| Surgeon Specialists | 500 |
| Enumerators | 10 |
| *Total allowed* | *25,000* |

*5 Leones = approx. US$1

## Per Diem Rates and Travel Allowance

Allowance is made for payments to community members as an incentive to attend council and other planning meetings. The per diem rate for attendance will be Le.10.00. Travelling allowance will be paid at the rate of Le.1.00/mile.

## Housing Allowance

The Provincial Director, CEAC and HCC leaders will be entitled to a housing allowance, when recruited out of their home bases, at the following rates:

Director:               400 Leones/month
Committee Leaders:      320 Leones/month

## Honorarium Payments

Ordinary members of CEAC and HCC will receive monthly honoraria for their services at the rate of Le.10/day. This will act as an incentive to do their best.

## Construction of Special Women's Health Centres

Provision is made, under office rents, for upgrading existing Health Care Centres while plans are being prepared for the construction of Special Centres. The Special Centres are estimated to have a minimum space of 10,000 square feet per centre. Current costs are estimated at Le.120 per square foot for this class of building, and construction is proposed to commence in the third year of the programme.

## Medical Supplies and Medical Equipment

The procurement of medical supplies and equipment will be centralized at the National Headquarters. Periodic requisition will be made by Provincial Councils to the Central Stores which will despatch supplies as requested. It is anticipated that the majority of the funds will come from foreign assistance.

## Office Supplies

These will be locally controlled. Provincial Councils will take advantage of locally produced materials and thus save costs of transportation of supplies from National Headquarters.

## Key Staff Positions and Qualifications Required

### 1) Professional Head
(Executive head of organization, responsible for co-ordination of the Council's programmes).
   A national, with either a Medical and MPH or a Social Sciences degree, with 10–15 years experience.

### 2) Chief Programme Adviser
Local, or foreign expert with international reputation. Must have Health Education/Public Health Degrees. Wide experience in African situations.

### 3) **Executive Health Office** (Seconded Staff)
Local with Medical degree and MPH, plus 7 years experience. Should have held senior administrative position in the MOH for minimum of 5 years.

### 4) **Education Welfare Office** (Seconded staff)
Local, with Social Service degree and 7 years experience. Must be a senior Welfare Officer with experience of provincial problems required.

### 5) **Education Officer** (Seconded staff)
Local, with Health Education qualification and 7 years experience in adult education programme. Should have had experience in rural education programmes.

### 6) **Publicity Officer** (responsible for co-ordination of publicity programmes all over the country)
Degree in Communications and 7 years experience. Knowledge of all provinces (or equivalent) of the country. Good practical knowledge of communication equipment.

### 7) **Provincial Director** (Head of Provincial Programmes)
National, with Medical degree. Must have wide experience in obstetrics and gynaecology with knowledge of the Province, including working knowledge of the principal local language. Some administrative experience required.

### 8) **Research Consultant** (Head of Research Unit)
Local expert, with Masters of Doctorate degree in Health Education. Competent researcher with wide experience in curriculum development and special adult programmes.

### 9) **Deputy Research Consultant**
Local medical expert with wide gynaecological specialization. Research experience. Should have current job in leadership position and be prepared to combine duties.

# Appendix 4

## FEMALE CIRCUMCISION
## STATEMENT OF *WHO* POSITION AND
## ACTIVITIES*

Female circumcision is a traditional practice which can have serious health consequences, and is of concern to the World Health Organization. Activities are carried out to combat this practice as part of its broader programmes of maternal and child health.

WHO [World Health Organization] supports the recommendations of the Khartoum Seminar of 1979 on Traditional Practices Affecting The Health of Women. These were that governments should adopt clear national policies to abolish female circumcision, and to intensify educational programmes to inform the public about the harmfulness of female circumcision. In particular, women's organizations at local levels are encouraged to be involved, since without women themselves being aware and committed, no changes are likely. In areas where female circumcision is still being practiced, women are also facing many other critical problems of ill health and malnutrition, lack of clean water, deaths in childbirth, overburden of work. These occur in extremely adverse social and economic circumstances. Surveys carried out recently with WHO support, also point to the continuing cultural and traditional pressures which perpetuate the practice. Programmes to combat harmful traditional practices, including female circumcision, should be seen within this context, and should respond sensitively to women's needs and problems.

WHO, together with UNICEF, has assured governments of its readiness to support national efforts against female circumcision, and to continue collaboration in research and dissemination of information. Special attention is given to the training of health workers at all levels, especially those for traditional birth attendants, midwives, healers and other practitioners of traditional medicine.

*Submitted to the U.N. Sub-Commission on Prevention of Discrimination and Protection of Minorities. Working Group on Slavery. Geneva, June 1982.

*WHO has consistently and unequivocally advised that female circumcision should not be practiced by any health professionals in any setting — including hospitals or other health establishments.*

Over the last five years the activities of WHO in respect of female circumcision have included preparation of informational material by staff members and consultants, particularly on the health consequences and the epidemiology of female circumcision; support to incorporate this material into appropriate training courses for various categories of health workers; technical and financial support to national surveys; convening the Khartoum Seminar referred to above; holding a consultation jointly with UNICEF to clarify and unify approaches; and publication of the proceedings of the Khartoum Seminar, including most recently the second volume which contains the papers presented at the Seminar.

# Appendix 5

## EXTRACT FROM A STATEMENT BY MR ABDOUL DIOUF, PRESIDENT OF THE REPUBLIC OF SENEGAL

Female mutilation is a subject that is taboo . . . But let us not rush into the error of condemning [genital mutilations] as uncivilized and sanguinary practices. One must beware of describing what is merely an aspect of difference in culture as barbarous. In traditional Africa, sexual mutilations evolved out of a coherent system, with its own values, beliefs, cultural and ritual conduct. They were a necessary ordeal in life because they completed the process of incorporating the child in society.

These practices, however, raise a problem today because our societies are in a process of major transformation and are coming up against new socio-cultural dynamic forces in which such practices have no place or appear to be relics of the past. What is therefore needed are measures to quicken their demise.

The main part of this struggle will be waged by education rather than by anathema and from the inside rather than from the outside. I hope that this struggle will make women free and "disalienated", personifying respect for the eminent dignity of life.

**Abdoul Diouf, 1985**

(Other African leaders who have made statements similar to President Diouf are the Presidents of Burkina Faso, Mr Thomas Sankara; of Benin, Mr Mathieu Kerekov; and of Kenya, Mr Daniel arap Moi. It helps those of us fighting FC to know that our leaders are sensitive to our sufferings. *O. Koso-Thomas*, 1987)

# The Inter-African Committee (IAC)

In 1984, the non-governmental organization (NGO) Working Group on Traditional Practices Affecting the Health of Women and Children, in collaboration with the Government of Senegal, the World Health Organization and UNICEF, organized a seminar in Dakar. Twenty African countries were represented by 100 participants.

In order to follow up the implementation of the recommendations of this Dakar seminar the Inter-African Committee was set up, and the co-ordinator of the NGO Working Group elected president. At both national and international levels, the IAC's activities against harmful traditional practices are mainly directed towards the practice of female circumcision. Several national and international organizations are engaged in conducting or supporting programmes aimed to sensitize women and men on the dangerous consequences of this practice.

National committees and other special bodies able to handle the problem in a manner acceptable to Africans are being created. These bodies conduct programmes of education, information and research, and are involved in various other activities relating to female circumcision. Meetings and seminars are organized in order to define strategies for fighting the practice.

At present the IAC has a secretariat in Dakar, operates a regional office in Addis Ababa, and maintains a liaison office in Geneva. National committees exist in: Djibouti, Egypt, Gambia, Ghana, Liberia, Mali, Nigeria, Senegal, Sudan and Togo. Groups/sections of the IAC working for the abolition of female circumcision among immigrants exist in France and England.

# Bibliography

## Books
El Dareer, Asma (1982) *Woman, Why do you Weep? Circumcision and its Consequences*. Zed Press, London.
*Encyclopedia Britannica*, 11th Edition "Circumcision" (historical origins) Vol. VI, pp. 1910–11. Cambridge University Press, UK.
Hall, H. U. (1938) *The Sherbro of Sierra Leone*. University of Pennsylvania Press, Philadelphia, USA.


## Reports, etc.
Anti-Slavery Society and *Radda Barnen* (Swedish Save the Children) *Female Circumcision*, public information pamphlet (October 1982). Revised, January 1984 by Special Committee of International NGO's on Human Rights, Geneva.
Bibiker Badria Scientific Association for Women's Studies, Omdurman, Sudan. Report on *African Women Speak* Workshop, Khartoum, October 1984.
Hosken, Fran, P. *The Hosken Report on Genital and Sexual Mutilation of Females*, (2nd Enlarged Edition) Women's International Network News, 1979.
Minority Rights Group Report No. 47, Scilla McLean, *Female Circumcision, Excision and Infibulation: the Fact, and Proposals for Change*, 1980.

NGO Inter-African Committee, Report of Seminar *Traditional Practices Affecting the Health of Women and Children in Africa*, Dakar, Senegal, February 1984.
UN Decade for Women Conference/Forum, Report of Workshops of NGO Inter-African Committee, Geneva on Traditional Practices Affecting the Health of Women and Children in Africa, Nairobi, July 1985.

UN, International Year of the Child Report No. 9, *Female Circumcision is a Health Hazard*, New York, 1979.
WHO Report, Gerald Zwang, *Female Sexual Mutilation – Technique and Results*, 1977.
WHO/EMRO Report, *Traditional Practices Affecting the Health of Women and Children*, Khartoum, February 1979.
WHO Global Review Paper from Khartoum Seminar, *Female Circumcision in the World Today*, March 1979 (WHO/EMRO Alexandria EM/SEM.TR.PR.AFF. HTH.WM/11).
WHO Background Papers for Seminar on *Traditional Practices Affecting the Health of Women and Children*. WHO/EMRO Technical Publication No. 2, Vol. 2, Alexandria. Edited by Dr R. H. O. Bannerman, Dr Hamid Rushwan and Mrs Iris Sharaf, 1982.

*Medical Dangers of Female Circumcision*, 1980.

Parliamentary proceedings preceding the law against female circumcision in the
United Kingdom. House of Lords, June 1983, *Circumcision Bills No. 1* and *No. 2*
(Lord Kennet).

A. M. Kamer, *Traditions and Superstitions among the Temne and Mende and the
Effect upon them of Western-type Education*. Thesis No. 97, Fourah Bay College,
Sierra Leone) 1964.